Dear

CW01629638

Hope you enjoy reading the book.

Best Regards.

Anusha Hansaria

10/09/2025

The Soul's Fuel

An Inspirational Collection for a Blissful life

Anusha Hansaria

16LEAVES

First Edition, 2023

www.instagram.com/bloggeratheart
www.twitter.com/AnushaHansaria

Paperback ISBN: 978-81-19221-28-8
eBook ISBN: 978-81-19221-23-3
WebPDF ISBN: 978-81-19221-27-1

Printed and bound in India by

16Leaves
2/579, Singaravelan Street
Chinna Neelankarai
Chennai - 600 041
India

info@16leaves.com
www.16Leaves.com
Call: 91-9940638999

This book is dedicated to my sister.
Thank you for making me realise that
I even ***have*** *a 'Philosophical' side to myself.*
Without you, this book wouldn't have existed

Acknowledgments

I would like to thank all the people that have ever crossed paths with me because this book is all about what life has taught me. Whenever you meet anyone, there is always some kind of learning that follows.

I would like to thank my father and mother, because parents are the most important source of almost everything that a child learns. A lot of the contents of this book are what they have taught me over the years. They have taught me how to see the positive in everything and that is what has helped me tremendously while writing this book.

I would like to thank my husband, for being my biggest critics as well as my biggest cheer-leader. I feel without having a critic, it is very difficult to improve. None of my blogs go forward without his approval, and I am so grateful for him.

I would also like to thank my sister, my in-laws and all my loved ones who read all my blogs and provide me motivation to write yet another. Thank you for keeping me going.

Above all, thank you God for giving me the ideas to write on and to help me take this first step towards fulfilling my dream.

Contents

Photo by Ilyass Seddoug on Unsplash

Actions Speak Louder Than Words

So always be mindful of your actions, and not just your words

This incident took place when I was studying in class 6 or 7 at the most. We had a school bus that would come to pick us up at a designated stop. This stop was around 2 kilometres away from my house, so I had to take a Rickshaw to and from the bus stop. A Rickshaw is basically a three wheeler vehicle found very commonly in many villages and towns of India. The front resembles a bicycle, whereas the rare part consists of two wheels and a seat on which two people could be seated at once. This passenger seat also has a shade on top of it to protect the passengers from getting wet in case of rain or to protect them from the direct sunlight. Since my timings were fixed, many times I would find the same vehicle that I had travelled in the previous day.

During a few of such trips, I began to observe a particular Rickshaw driver always waiting for me, and he would always place his vehicle such that he would be the first one I would cross. Initially, I didn't pay any heed to it, thinking it just to be a coincidence. It started bothering me when I started observing him waiting for me when I would get back from school as well. I would even observe him refuse a few other passengers who would ask for his service.

Slowly, it began to give me the creeps. There was something about his behaviour that made me feel on edge. So one such day, I decided to take a different Rickshaw when I got back from school, even though I had seen him waiting for me. I was flabbergasted to see him cycle his empty Rickshaw at full speed and overtake the one I was sitting in. He didn't stop though, and just drafted past me. I was just trying to take in what had just happened when I saw him waiting a few steps from my house. He was standing on the road looking intently as my Rickshaw drew closer, and his forehead was creased. Just then, as my Rickshaw passed him, he kicked a small stone in my direction. It thankfully didn't hit the Rickshaw or me, but it was enough to convey his anger. I was dead scared and raced inside my house as soon as I reached and told my parents all about it. They then filed a police complaint of the same, and thankfully, that was the last I saw of him.

Though he had never said a single word to me ever, his actions and body language were enough to scare me to death. It was sufficient to warn me about some unknown harm.

...

You are on a first date with some guy you met on maybe say a dating site. You place your order, and you start talking. He keeps nodding while you speak, but you can feel that he isn't completely into the conversation. You can notice him fidgeting with his fingers or taping his feet, or even notice his eyes darting elsewhere every now and then. Would you want to go on a second date with this person?

He may have said all the right things throughout the date, but his actions did not match his words. Though he tried to show you that he is interested, his actions gave him away. That's how important actions are. Just his actions made you realize that he isn't the one for you.

Why is body language so important? Why does an interviewer always keep a keen eye on your body language and not just on your answers? It is because your body doesn't lie. You may unknowingly do something that may directly contradict the answer that you give to a question. By observing your body language, an interviewer can figure out how much truth is being spoken. A lot can be judged about a person by just observing his body language.

Words are often compared to a sword. It's that deep a wound words can inflict. But, your actions are no less. Just like words, actions can hurt a person equally. By action, I don't mean physically hurting a person; it is rather your body language and your facial expression which can also hurt a person to unknown levels.

Let's try to recall about a time when our parents may have asked us regarding any basic functionality of a smartphone. We may not have said anything to them directly, but more often than not, we may think it to be such a silly question and even wonder how they could not have known this. While we don't say anything verbally, our body does react to our thoughts. We may, unknowingly, display our dislike through our body language or by our facial expression; for example, as simple an action as rolling our eye. This action, though, makes it abundantly clear to the other person what we are thinking.

We need to be more mindful of our actions near kids because they can sense it much more than grown-ups. When a child is hurt by someone's actions, it may leave a wound on its heart for a lifetime, a wound that will never heal. A simple action may have drastic effects on a child, and it may mould its entire future differently. Before a child is able to speak, it communicates only through actions. A child is always most comfortable with someone it feels safe and loved.

When we feel extreme anger towards our child, sometimes along with scolding, we may jerk them a little, not exactly hard enough to cause them pain but to show our disapproval. We may not realise, but more than the scolding, this action is what hurts them more. It makes them feel unwanted and unloved. This is something we should never do. No matter how angry we may be, we shouldn't let a child ever feel that it's not loved because that hurt is too brutal for the tiny soul. We should explain it what was wrong, but in a loving way.

Love can make a child understand its mistake faster than hurting them or scolding them ever will. After all, that's why they are called children. They need to be taught what's right and wrong in a loving way and not by anger. Because, love is the most beautiful language which we can used to communicate our thoughts; not just with a child, but with anyone.

What we can do to help ourselves to be more mindful of our actions is that we can try to understand the various aspects of body language. There are several books and trainings that we may undergo to understand the concept of body language better. It is one of the most important soft skills that we may gift ourselves, which will help us in all aspects of our lives. It will help you personally as well as professionally.

One of the best quotes that I have come across that explains the importance of actions over words goes as follows:

> *"If your actions don't live up to your words, you have nothing to say."*
>
> – DaShanne Stokes

Can That First Love Happen Twice?

Do you ever forget your
first true love?

Photo by Farrinni on Unsplash

You are in love with someone and imagine your entire life with that special person. You are happy and sure that you have found your soul-mate. But then, life brings such obstacles on your way in which you have to make the difficult choice of letting go of your love and getting on with your life. Initially, it is very difficult, and you never expect you will ever be able to overcome that pain, the pain of that heartbreak. But gradually, time does heal all types of wounds and you begin to live life again, even if not for yourself, but for your loved ones because seeing them worry about you is just not possible to bear. Another important factor is that it doesn't change the fact that life goes on and we are forced to move on with it.

As life goes by, you find the perfect companion for yourself and get married. At this point, the main factor you look for is companionship and not love exactly. Love seems to take a backseat. You may find the best companion in your life-partner, but is it ever possible to fall in love again?

If you ever happen to cross paths with your ex; who you were really in love with but you just couldn't spend the rest of your life with because of some unavoidable circumstances, doesn't your heart still miss a beat? Don't you still wonder how life would have been if you could have been successful at love?

But being successful at love is only granted to those few lucky ones. Most people are forced to choose life over true love.

Why is it called first love? It is because true love happens only once. It isn't necessary that the first boyfriend/girlfriend you had were your first love. It may just have been an attraction or an infatuation. When we are young, we do get attracted to the opposite sex and what we believe to be love may actually not be love. Sometimes, it does take a few failed relationships before we really understand what love actually is, and we understand this only when we do experience it. This true love is what is called first love.

However, it is not necessary that if we find our true love and life happens to be so grateful that we get to marry this person, it will be a happily ever after. Life isn't that simple, most of the time. For a marriage to work, there are a lot of factors that come into play. Some of them are – companionship, respect, trust, understanding, commitment, and patience among several others; among which love is just a very tiny insignificant factor.

A marriage without true love may still be successful, but it is very difficult to make a marriage work with only true love. That's the reason why we see more number of love marriages ending in divorce as compared to arranged marriages.

Though we always crave to find that true love of our life, what we fail to understand is that, true love is just good to be read in stories or to be watched in movies – be an audience to it. Actually, witnessing it may destroy you. You can compare it to the Sun: It is beautiful to look at – the sunrise, the sunset, or even when it is directly overhead shining brightly in the sky and making everything around it look alive and beautiful, it looks simply mesmerizing to look at; but if you even try to go near it, it will burn you to ashes. It is just meant to be admired from afar. Similarly, even true love seems to be better to be admired for a safe distance, since even coming near it may leave you heartbroken for the rest of your life. So, doesn't it seem better to never witness true love than to have to bear the pain of being heartbroken? Maybe that's why God saves some of us from finding that true love.

First Love has been quite accurately described in the quote below:

> *"First love is a kind of vaccination that immunizes a man from catching the disease a second time."*
>
> Honoré de Balzac

Photo by Pierre Bamin on Unsplash

Why Do We Need Friends?

Family is important, but friends are important too…

When a child is born, in a few months, it starts to recognize its parents. These are the first people a child gets familiar with. Gradually, it starts to recognize its immediate family and close relatives it is introduced to.

Slowly, the child grows up a little and starts going to play school. That is the first time it finds itself between other kids of its age. Gradually, it gets comfortable with a few of them, but at this time, the concept of friendship is not something it understands.

Next phase of a child's life is when it starts going to a proper school. This is the time when the child starts making friends (the few ones with whom it feels comfortable and connected with, though its young mind is still too young to grasp the depth of the word 'Friends'). At this point, it is just someone it always plays with or maybe sits next to during class.

When we are small, we make many such friends. When we are in primary classes, very few find such friends with whom they stick for life. I used to have new friends every year when I was promoted to the next class. Being an introvert, I would find it difficult to start a conversation with any other batch mate, and it would usually be my bench-mate with whom I would hang out during breaks and think of as my friend.

As I grew older, I started making a few more friends (friends who wouldn't change yearly). Towards the end of school life, we thought we would always keep in touch with these few friends that we made, but that as we know it, is better said than done. I changed my city for my higher education, and slowly, we all got busy with our new lives and new friends. This is the phase where I made few true friends who were to be kept for a lifetime. You don't need to put in any extra effort for it; you just know it when you do find someone like that.

As you go on with your life, a number of changes takes place – You start working and find yourself extremely busy, change cities for better job opportunities and even get married in a completely different city (like in my case), far away from these treasures that we found on this journey of life. But these friends are different. These friends are the ones who you may not talk to or meet every day, but you know they are there for you and whenever we do get that privilege to meet them or even just talk to them, they seem to heal you in unspoken ways.

Now, why do you think we need friends? Friends are the ones who fulfil that missing piece in each other's life, which helps to make this life a little more bearable and liveable. The ones we make friends with are the ones who fulfil this missing piece in our life, and similarly, we fulfil that missing piece in theirs. It is like two broken pieces that complete each other, thus helping each other go on with this difficult and ruthless life. They fit in such a way that when you are with them, life may even seem beautiful. They are the medicine that's required to lead a healthy and normal life, the types which you cannot skip even on your lazy days.

Husband and wife are known as soul mates that complete each other. Having that true friend, I believe, is also like having a soul mate - they complete you in ways we may not know.

...

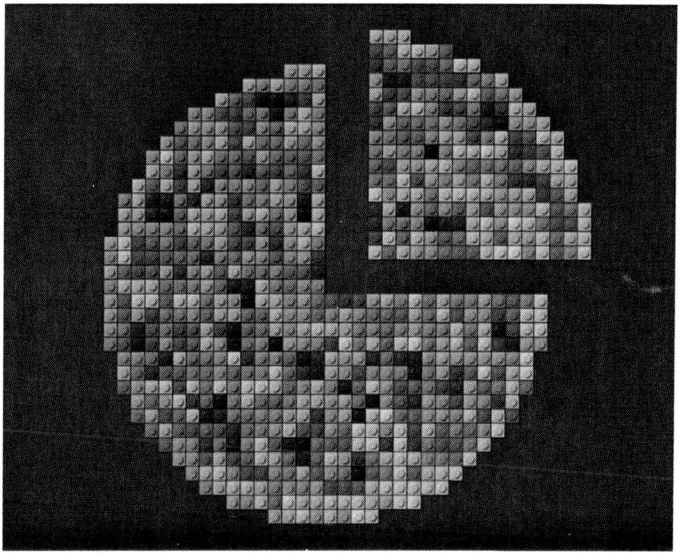

Photo by Vadim Bogulov on Unsplash

All types of friends are important. Together, they help to complete the several missing parts in us and make us whole. To complete a jigsaw puzzle, it is necessary to have all the tiny little pieces. Even a single missing piece can make a huge difference as the puzzle will never look complete. You cannot even try and fit in any other puzzle piece in its place, this is how much importance every tiny piece holds.

Similarly in life, we require all types of friends to complete us in different ways.

There may be a few friends with whom you love to party, which just refreshes you and helps you to carry on in life; then there are the ones with whom you connect emotionally, just talking to them or even a tight hug from them is enough to provide you the strength that you need – It helps you get rid of the pain that you hold in your heart to a great extent; then you have your office buddies because of whom you look forward to going to office – you can just rant out all the office related frustrations in front of them and know that it's safe with them, and just having them listen, makes it feel better.

Talking and sharing your emotions with someone who understands you are very important. It is like meditation. Sharing any life problems with someone doesn't mean that they can help it go away; it is the emotional support they provide that helps us feel strong enough to face it and go on with it. Many times, it is our spouses, parents, or siblings who we share these with, but every relationship has its own limitations. There are different things you share with different people, and there are various reasons for it.

For example, there may be a few things which you cannot share with your parents or siblings, simply because you know that they always want to see you happy. Letting them have even a hint that it is not the case, will hurt them tremendously. So, to rid them of this pain, you tend to keep it within yourself. But, not sharing our emotions with anyone, just piles on inside us which can result in several health issues and just tends to destroy us.

This is when the importance of having friends, along with family, steps in. These are the feelings and emotions we tend to share with our close friends, and just sharing all your difficulties with each other makes us feel the emotional wound we all carry in our hearts, begin to heal. It doesn't mean that it doesn't hurt them to know that something is preventing you from being happy – after all, even they love you the way your family does. The difference is just that even they are in similar situation. Life is difficult for everyone and everyone needs that shoulder where they can lean on. When we share our pain with our friends, it is both ways. Even they share theirs with us, and this way, we both help each other generate the strength required to go on with life.

Friends are those who don't judge you, just like your family. That's why these special ones are said to be our siblings from another mother, because they are like family to us. They know you in and out, and you can be yourself around them. They provide you with that comfort, which is in knowing that you can share anything and everything with them, yet they will always love you. They just love you for being 'You'.

One very good quote that I feel accurately describes the importance of having friends, goes as below:

> *"A friend knows the song in my heart and sings it to me when my memory fails."*
>
> – Donna Roberts

Photo by Khadeeja Yasser on Unsplash

Is Being Punctual A Blessing Or A Curse?

Flexibility is the key

"Better three hours too soon than a minute late"
William Shakespeare

"Punctuality is the first step towards Success"
Nishtunishaa

We all have heard these famous sayings at some or the other point in our lives, right? We have always been made to understand the importance of being punctual by our parents and our teachers at school since we were kids, and I totally vouch for it. Even in our professional lives, we are always expected to be on time and made to realize its worth. People tend to value the person who values time since this is the person who has already understood the most important aspect of life, and nothing can stop him from achieving success.

I believe the person who understands the importance of time can achieve anything in life. They are the ones who can manage their time to the best of their abilities and reach the goal they have set for themselves in life. Every minute is important and shouldn't be wasted deliberately. We can achieve a lot in a minute as well; aren't we made to realize that a minute isn't a small amount of time when we do planks? God, that single minute!!!

When we go for job interviews, we always try to reach the place before the scheduled time so that we don't miss the opportunity. However, I am sure most of us have experienced that the interview doesn't start on time, and we are made to wait for hours sometimes. That is a very big turn-off factor for me because if the candidate's time is not valued, do you think they are going to value you as an employee of their company? Moreover, it shows the unprofessionalism of the company.

So, punctuality says a lot about a person (or an organization in this case).

Having said that, I also feel that as much as having punctuality as a virtue is important (it is a blessing); being flexible is also equally important.

Why I sometimes wonder if it is a curse is because I have seen people who follow punctuality as a religion and get extremely upset when the other is not able to meet that standard. They don't even give the person an opportunity to reason themselves out. I feel it is necessary to give the other person a chance to explain the reason, and then, you are the best judge to decide if the delay was genuine or not.

In today's world, there are so many uncertainties. When we commit to anything, it is always to the best of our capabilities. But, as humans, it is not in our hands to foresee any unavoidable situations that may arise, and it may cause hurdles for us to complete our commitments in the deadline we had set. In such a situation, the best thing another person can do for someone is to listen. Lend your ear to the person and try to understand what may have caused the delay.

While there are few whose nature is to delay the task at hand and just come up with vague reasons for the delay, every person is not the same. Some people are genuine when they give a reason for the delay, and the most they ask of you is to just give them a chance to explain themselves. Those few minutes which you may spend on listening and reasoning, may just help someone in ways you may never even contemplate.

Life is difficult. If we may help a person in any way possible, we must try and grab that opportunity. As we have heard, what goes around comes around. So, the good we do for others always comes back to us in different ways. Along with this, even the satisfaction we feel when we are able to help a person in need, in any way, is worth all of it.

The quote below perfectly explains the importance of flexibility in life:

> *In all matters, moderation is desirable. If a thing is carried to excess, it will prove a source of evil.*
>
> – Bahá'u'lláh

Too much of anything is bad. If we overdo anything that is good, the outcome may not always be good. A simple example – we all know that we should include nuts in our diet (especially vegetarians) as it is a rich source of protein. But, if we eat too much of it, it does produce excess heat in our body, which may lead to several health issues.

> *Therefore, balance is always required.* ***Flexibility*** *is the key to a happy and peaceful life.*

Photo by Andre Taissin on Unsplash

Sometimes Ignorance Is Bliss

Knowing things may sometimes prove to be more painful than actually being ignorant about it

While growing up, we used to live in a joint family, which consisted of everyone from my grandfather to my uncles and their respective families. As my grandfather grew older, he slowly started losing his hearing powers, as is common with old age. So, my father got him a hearing aid to help him cope with his hearing problem. But, he just used it for the initial few days, and then he stopped using it completely. He would always come up with some reason or the other for not using it. I couldn't understand the reason for it at that time. My little brain just couldn't contemplate why anyone would prefer not want to hear everything that was happening around them when they had an option and instead bear the inconvenience.

As I grew older, I started to get acquainted with what we call 'Life', and as we all have witnessed it on multiple occasions, it can get really tough at times. You meet all types of people and face all types of possible situations in this journey. Some experiences are good, and some may cause us immense pain. All these experiences (whether good or bad) get stored in our brain in the form of memories, and we just can never seem to forget about them, especially the painful ones.

More often than not, these painful memories consist of some actions but mainly words that seem to just prick our hearts like a sharp knife, which can never be healed. Just imagine, if for some reason, we weren't able to hear those hurtful words being spoken, wouldn't we have been able to rid ourselves of at least a tiny amount of pain?

All these years later, that is what I learned, and I was finally able to understand why my grandfather preferred not to wear the hearing aid. He just felt more at peace, not having to hear everything that was going around him, and instead preferred to keep his mind occupied with better things, and make the best out of the few years that he had left.

...

It is actually a bliss not knowing what people think about you. It is really none of your concerns, or any of your business. As far as they treat you properly, you shouldn't bother what they actually think about you or what is being said behind your back. You can't control it anyway, can you? And moreover, we can't dictate anyone as to what they are allowed to think or speak about us.

People can be horrible if they want to for no logical reason at all.

Getting to know any horrible feeling that someone may hold towards you will only bring you pain. Is life not tough enough as it is? Why should we invite more pain?

Isn't it better to be ignorant about the ones those we can avoid.

In one of the most loved series – Friends – there is a character from it named Phoebe. There is this one episode where they show that when Phoebe was young and her mother was still alive, her mother used to show her just the happy parts of the movies and switch it off before the sad endings and made her believe that life is full of just the beautiful things. It was just her way of protecting her daughter from the pain and distress of life for as long as it was possible for her. She didn't want to break her little girl's heart by letting her know how cruel life could be. She let her daughter be ignorant so that she could be happy and love life the way it is.

As we grow older, life teaches us everything and also gives us the strength to deal with it in its weird ways. So, it isn't always a wrong thing to keep someone ignorant of some information that will only cause them to hurt. But we do need to seriously judge the fact that by hiding any such information; we aren't causing them any harm in any way.

...

Some people have hereditary diseases, which may not cause any harm, but they just have it. Do you think them knowing about it will make any difference? Many hereditary illnesses have no cure and don't really cause a lot of inconvenience in the person's day-to-day life. Leading a healthy life is the best they can do. *Once they get a name to their condition, it just makes it worse.*

People then tend to link every single thing they may feel with the illness and increase their blood pressure for no reason. They tend to Google about the disease, and as we all know it, Google provides the worst-case scenario that may happen for any diseases. This leads the person to take excess stress and tension, which actually makes the person ill rather than the actual illness.

This way, the person harms themself much more than the actual illness would, unknowingly.

In such cases, don't you feel it would have been best if the person would have been ignorant regarding any hereditary illness he may have and instead, just get any symptom treated that he may witness, as and when required?

It is not required to know about all the hereditary illnesses you may have until unless there are some precautions that you may incorporate in your life to keep yourself healthy. One such example may be that if your parents are diabetic, it would be better to control your sugar intake and get regular tests done to monitor your sugar levels. But, except for a few such hereditary diseases, all other hereditary illnesses are not necessarily required to be aware of if we want to keep our sanity in place.

...

Though there are several things in life that we ought to know to prepare ourselves and deal with it better, few things are best to be ignorant of.

Just enjoy your life to the fullest and deal with it in the best way you can.

One very meaningful quote that I completely agree with goes as follows:

> *The only reason the world was a better place during your childhood is because you were a child.*
>
> J.R. Rim

Importance Of Reading

Helps you live in so many different worlds at once

Photo by Matias North in Unsplash

When I was in school, every week we would have one 40 minutes class, where we were taken to the school library and we had to pick any novel of our liking. We were then required to read this novel and return it the following week. If we were not able to finish reading the novel in that one week's duration, we could opt for taking the same novel home again for another week.

Now the catch here was that we were actually expected to read it. Whenever we used to return the novel, the Ma'am (who used to manage the library), would call anyone of us randomly, and we would have to give a summary of the story of the novel we had just returned. This was her way of checking that we had read the novel, which would help cultivate our reading habit.

During those days, reading novels were not really my cup of tea. I loved to listen to stories – YES, but reading them myself, was a complete no. Luckily for me, my elder sister was a bookworm. So, every week, I would ask her preferences on which novel she would like to read, and I would pick that up during my library class and give it to her on coming back home. She would then read it, and tell me the story before my next library class was due, so that I would not get caught and punished for not reading it.

This was our secret setting which was a win-win situation for both of us.

So, during my entire school life, I did not even read a single novel. I used to read comics, yes, but reading an entire book with just one story in it, was something I just could not contemplate how anyone could find that interesting.

...

Soon, I started with my college and for that; I had to move to a completely new city. I used to stay in a hostel and on my floor, we were ten of us. But, as luck would have it, among the ten of us, the other nine were in the same stream and I was the only odd one out.

Though that did not affect us in becoming the best of friends in the years to come, but their college timings were completely different from mine, and I found myself alone in the entire floor more often than I would really hope for.

It was during that time that I purchased my first novel. No one still believes me when I tell them that I actually took six whole months to finish my first novel, but that is true!! Maybe my choice of the novel (to be my first) was not actually correct as I just could not keep myself glued to it for long. But things really changed after that.

The next novel I purchased; I feel was what initiated my love for reading. It was so addictive, that I just could not keep it down once I started it, and I finished the entire novel at one go and finally went to bed at 4 in the morning!! Time just flew by and I was so engrossed on the story, I lost track of time and the fact that I had college the next day and so I had to sleep. It was then that I discovered which genre my interest lied in.

Since then, I have been a bookworm myself, and I would say, it was the best thing to have ever happened to me.

...

Reading did help me in several ways, like – when I had a bad phase going on during my hostel life, I read a lot of novels during that time. It helped me escape the toxic environment for the hours I would be engrossed in the storyline, and live a completely different life. The line between reality and fiction would fade, and it really helped me navigate through that difficult phase.

Even now, novels are my escape route: it helps me escape anything unpleasant happening in my life and get lost in the world of imagination.

But that is not the only thing reading helps us in. Whenever I read any book, I really admire the use of words and the way writers describe abstract things, so much so that you feel you can see the entire scene unfold right in front of your eyes. It helps us improve our vocabulary. I also believe, reading all these novels in all these years are what have helped me to pen down my thoughts into the exact words. I find myself to be able to express a lot better in writing, as compared to speaking.

Another thing that reading helps us in is, to increase our knowledge about so many things. For example, whenever we read any novel, we get to know about the place the story is based in, their culture, and their lifestyle, which we, otherwise, would have never come across.

Reading is one of the best hobbies one can cultivate. We just need to figure out where our interests lies in, and once we understand that, cultivating the habit of reading is never going to be a challenging task.

One quote that I really vouch for goes as follows:

> *The greatest gift is a passion for reading.*
>
> Elizabeth Hardwick

There Is Always A New Beginning

Age is never a factor when it comes to starting something afresh

Photo by Jukan Tateisi on Unsplash

I was the first one to get placed from my college through campus recruitment, and that too at the world's third best organization to work for. As you all may guess, I was on cloud nine; as were my parents, friends and so was the person in-charge of the college placement, as this would have a good impact on the college reputation.

Life just seemed to have changed for me overnight.

From that day forth, everyone in the college seemed to know me. Whenever I used to go to wish luck to my friends before any Company's Aptitude test, everyone used to tease me to not take the test and let them get a chance to get placed instead. I would have to explain that I was just there to wish luck and nothing more.

I was looked upon as the luckiest girl whose life was set for a lifetime. Without doubt, I felt the same that time. It was a dream come true and I couldn't be more grateful for it.

Life just seemed so perfect.

Soon, it was my first day at the Company and I fell in love with it at the very first sight. The office was so huge and so beautiful. I had already decided to work at this company for my entire life on the first day itself – that is how impressed I was with it.

Everything just seemed like a fairy-tale.

The first two years just flew by at a blink of an eye. But, unfortunately, then started the office politics. I, being very new to this world, couldn't take it for long. After few more months of trying to adjust, I decided this wasn't what I wanted for life. Finally, I resigned from what I thought was my dream job, without any other offer at hand.

All at once I was jobless.

I started hunting for another job, but to my horror, I realized that it wasn't that easy to get a decent job. I was looking for a job on the same technology I had worked on in the previous organization, but I found out that there weren't many opportunities on the same.

I had also forwarded my CV to all my college friends so that they could refer me for any openings in the companies they were working in. Days passed onto months and slowly it was almost a year since I had resigned from my first job.

I faced countless rejections during this time and was on the verge of giving up.

Just then, one night, one of my college friends messaged me to inform that there was an opening at his company, but it was for fresher level and the salary was very basic.

Also, the technology that I would have to work on wouldn't be the same, but they would provide training. It would be like starting afresh. Since, I had given up all hopes of landing a job at all, I immediately informed him I was very interested, without even giving it another thought, and thanked him profoundly.

The interview process started the very next day, and by God's grace, I got selected for the same. I was to move to another city for 5 months during which period we would be given training on a new technology, and then, based on the requirement, we would be posted to any of their offices, which could be in any city in the entire country.

Since, I didn't have any other option, I took up this opportunity that was presented to me at the time when I was almost about to give up. Hence, this was the starting of my 'second' new beginning, that too at a completely new place and between completely unknown people.

I had made up my heart; I would give this job all that it takes.

I paid attention during the trainings, and during the free time that I got, I enjoyed my life with my new colleagues.

The city being on the coastal region, had loads of opportunities for weekend getaways. So, during weekends, we would plan short trips around the city and its adjoining places. These short trips helped us to re-energize our minds and we made friends those were to keep for a lifetime.

Soon, the 5 months came to an end, and we were to give tests on all the trainings that we had received. I did quite well and was awarded for being the overall topper of the batch.

Soon, I was placed at a different city with few more of my colleagues.

It was just a week that I had started working at this new office when, my marriage got fixed and was to take place just after 2 months. On top of that, after marriage I was to relocate to another city – where my husband was located.

Though I was happy for my marriage, it pained me to think of the fact that I would have to give up the job that I had worked so hard for in these last 5 months and had come to love it.

I knew that after marriage, it wouldn't be possible to find a job on the current technology that I was working on, since I just had the training to talk about and no real work experience. It was clear to me that my married life was going to mark yet another new beginning for me.

Soon I got married, and the initial few months just flew by in a blurry train of events. This time, I wasn't even much keen on starting my career once again from the very beginning, when I already had around 3 years of work experience.

Above all, I was scared; scared if I would again be able to find a job of my liking, scared of again joining as a fresher where the other fresher's would be much younger (and maybe smarter) than me, scared of failure.

It had already been 6 months to my marriage, and I decided to stay as a housewife and give up my career for good, when my husband strongly encouraged me to do any crash-course of my interest that would help me in getting a job.

It was the little push I needed at that moment. After a lot of research, and since I have always had interest in coding, I decided to do a certification course on Android.

Once that was over, I, once again, started my job hunt for a fresher's profile. After a plentiful of rejections, I finally got an offer from a small start-up.

When I say small, I feel I should mention that if I decided to join it, I would be the only employee in it, and the pay was obviously very minimal since they were not a funded start-up till then.

I heard about the project idea that the owner had, and it somehow interested me. I knew I would get to learn a lot and I guess that is what made me take up the offer.

Since then, I guess I took several right choices at the right time by God's grace, and looking back, I feel I am exactly where I was meant to be.

Though till date I have had several new beginnings, I feel what helped me was that I did go ahead with each one of them (of course with lots of encouragement and support from my family and friends, and above all, the Almighty). Had I been scared and given up, I would never have been able to achieve my dream.

Though there are several people younger than me who have achieved a lot more than I have, in some companies I have even had team leads who had lesser total years of experience than I did, but everyone's path is different, right?

Each one of us has led a different life and has a different story, and we should aim at doing the best we can with our life, without comparing it with others.

We shouldn't hesitate to take up any good opportunities that life gives us. If we can be sure that we have giving in our best in life, best of our capabilities, then we should be content with what we have achieved and pat our backs and say, *"Well Done"*.

Above all, always remember, it is never too late for a New Beginning.

One good quote that I try to live by, goes as follows:

> *"Celebrate endings—for they precede new beginnings."*
>
> Jonathan Lockwood Huie

The Un-owned Painting

The unknown factor making it all the more mysterious and beautiful

Photo by Anusha Hansaria

My husband and I had just finished the tedious process of renovating our home and were in the process of decorating it, when we heard the doorbell ring. On opening the door we found that someone had sent us a parcel but there was neither any sender's name nor any return address mentioned, where the parcel could be returned in case it was unable to be delivered.

As we flipped the parcel back and forth to find the sender's name or address, the delivery guy started getting impatient since he had loads of other deliveries to complete before the day got over. So, we had to take the parcel and sign the receipt form, and not waste any more of his time. We were sure that it must be from any one of our relatives or friends and soon we would get to know about the sender.

Now, as we were extremely excited and no longer able to contain the surprise any longer, we quickly un-wrapped the parcel, to find a beautiful painting inside. The colours used in it were just amazing and the art in it left us to fully utilize our imagination to try and understand what the painting was trying to depict. I even found the perfect spot and hung the painting there, with no further delay. It seemed like it was made exactly for that particular spot. It looked just beautiful.

Soon, days passed by and it was almost a month since we had received that un-owned painting (now, that is what I started referring it to as). We just couldn't figure out who could this person is, and without even a vague idea about the sender, we couldn't really ask anyone. We couldn't do anything but to wait for someone to inquire if we have received it. After all, I couldn't fathom the fact that anyone could just send such a beautiful painting and want to keep themself as a secret sender!

As the days passed by further, we started getting more and more mysterious about the painting. At one instance, I also imagined it to have some kind of inbuilt spy camera that we see in movies. This thought was, however, soon rubbished by me since I realize that there actually won't be any benefit for anyone to spy on us. After all, neither my husband nor I held on to any secret data that could be crucial to anyone.

As the days turned to months, we finally gave up on trying figuring out the sender of the un-owned painting. After all, if the sender wanted to be known, he/ she would have informed us already by now, so it was of no use for us to give it any more of a thought.

Till the present date, the painting still hangs on the exact same spot, adding beauty to the area, and with all the mysteries still hidden within it.

As rightly expressed:

> *It's the unknown that draws people.*
>
> — E.A. Bucchianeri, *Brushstrokes of a Gadfly, (Gadfly Saga, #1)*

...

Thinking about the beauty and mysteries associated with this un-owned painting, isn't there something that's exactly like it — beautiful, yet full of mysteries? Yes, you are correct — Life. We can never say who actually own our life; we don't have any control over it, do we? We may be laughing at one moment but, at the very next moment, we don't really know what may happen. When we go to sleep at night after a long and hectic day, can we guarantee that we are going to wake up the next day? We plan so many things for our future, but can we be sure we will be there to live that future?

Though life is so unpredictable, yet it is beautiful. Like they say live life to the fullest at the present moment because, you never know how long you have been granted this beautiful life for.

Wear all those new pretty clothes that you have kept lock up in your cupboard, waiting for that perfect occasion to wear them. Look your best every day, because you never know which your last is. Don't let any of your wishes go unfulfilled, if you have the privilege of living them today. Most importantly, don't forget to thank God every night for granting you this day, and every morning because He helped you wake up to yet another day full of opportunities.

We should enjoy the unknown and admire the beauty of our un-owned life, just like the un-owned painting.

It's Time To Let Go...

Don't keep that burden in your heart forever

Photo by Gianandrea Villa on Unsplash

When I was a little girl, I used to be very weak physically; but that didn't stop me from fighting with my elder sibling. As soon as our father would head out of the door and leave for his office, our fight would start. It would usually start with me irritating my elder sister (that's what younger siblings usually does, isn't it?). But, in our case the ending would be a little different. When my sister would be completely pissed, she would hit me to make me stop doing the thing that was irritating her. I, on the other hand, being weak physically, wouldn't be able to match her strength. Instead, I would use the most effective strength that I had and would work every time —crying and blackmailing her. Once I would start crying, she would do anything possible to make me laugh and make sure that I didn't complain about it to my father once he would be back from office.

She knew that if our father got to know, she would get a good thrashing from him for hitting me and making me cry. Firstly because, I was too weak to fight her like equals, that he believed to be unfair; and secondly, he used to believe, that since I was her younger sibling, she should deal with me with more patience and love. She knew that father wouldn't be concerned with what I did to enrage her at the first place. He, being the eldest among his siblings, had always treated all his younger sisters and brothers with a lot of love, and he expected the same from her. Moreover, she knew how much our father hated to walk into the house, after a hectic day of work, just to find me crying.

So, in order to avoid all the mess that would follow, she would try to make up for hitting me. That would be anything ranging from intentionally singing the wrong lyrics of a song to make me laugh, giving me something of hers that I had my eyes on, and if none of these worked, she would ultimately surrender herself to me. When I say surrender herself, it would mean that she would make me sit on the bed and she would sit on the floor (so that I would have easy access to her, since, she was not only stronger but also taller than me), and then I could either pull her hair or scratch her with my nails, to help me take out all my anger till I was satisfied that the punishment would suffice the fact that she hit me and caused me pain.

Now, whenever I think about those days, it makes me extremely sad and guilty to the point that I hate myself for causing her so much pain. Many times I find myself praying to God to shower so much happiness into her life so that it erases the pain that I had caused her when we were little. I can't seem to forgive myself for the inhuman behaviour on my part. I keep hoping for ways that I could somehow undo whatever pain I had caused her, or shake my younger self till I could push some sense inside so that I could have seen how insensitive I was being for misusing the fact of me being physically weak. It just feels so wrong.

Most of us have some or the other regrets in life. Something we wish we hadn't done and would love to change if given even the tiniest of opportunities. We all have been there, haven't we? Deep inside, we all know there is nothing that can be done now to change it; yet, we visit that corner of our brain and sadden ourselves over it. It is like living the phrase – crying over spilled milk.

If someone do us wrong, but, if they later realize their mistake and ask for our forgiveness, we usually try and forgive them. We may not forget what they did, but knowing the fact that they do realise their mistake and they have found the strength to say sorry and make amends for it, we do forgive them for it, don't we? After all that is what we have been taught and it is what we would love to teach our children.

When we can forgive others for hurting us in any way, why is it so difficult to forgive our own selves for hurting someone else? Don't we deserve our own forgiveness when we do realise our mistakes? Why is it so hard to forgive oneself? Why do we always hold on to a memory that causes us pain? Why is it so difficult to just let it go?

The main reason why we just can't seem to let go, according to me, is the fact that we always expect the best from ourselves. The things we idolize are the things we expect ourselves to be. Then, when we commit any mistake, it just makes it hard for us to accept the fact that we have done something wrong, and thus, just makes it impossible for us to forgive and forget.

What we need to understand is that even we are human, and it is human nature to make mistakes. We should make amends for it, that is for sure, but once we have done that, we need to let it go and free ourselves from its burden. We don't need to be so strict with ourselves. Just like others, we do deserve our own forgiveness once we realize our mistake and are ready to rectify it. Isn't that what forgiveness is all about.

Forgiving oneself is the toughest of all, and once we have reached that stage, life will seem so beautiful. We will be more at ease mentally and be able to admire our surroundings with a clearer view. That is what we need to aim for. We need to start treating ourselves as we treat others and then we will see that the world will become such a lovely place to live in. As then, nobody would ever hurt the other intentionally.

One of the most beautiful quotes that I have come across, that explain the importance of letting go, goes as follows:

"Accept yourself, love yourself, and keep moving forward. If you want to fly, you have to give up what weighs you down."

— Roy T. Bennett, *The Light in the Heart*

Photo by Wolfgang Hasselmann on Unsplash

Little Things...

They matter the most in life

You are in one of your regular morning walks; you cross a lot of people on the park that are walking, jogging or doing some or the other form of exercises. Your eyes meet the eyes that of a stranger and the stranger smiles. It instantly brings a smile on your face in return and lightens up your mood. It makes you feel good for no particular reason.

Once back home, you get ready for work. During the entire process you have a smile on your face, a song playing on your lips and you are in a good mood just because of that sweet gesture from the stranger.

You reach your office and take the elevator to your floor. There is one more person in the lift whom you may not know. Because of your elated mood, you greet the person with a little cheerful hello. You can feel the entire composer of the person change as he/she greets you back. You have now shared that happiness within you with this other stranger and helped elate his/her mood as well. Your happiness doesn't reduce, instead it adds on seeing the other person reflect your greeting. Happiness is contagious in that way.

What the first stranger did in the park was just a small sweet gesture, but he unknowingly helped to create a chain of sweet gestures in return, and thus elating the mood of several others. Had he not bothered to smile back at you, your day could have been just the same as the rest of your days.

You don't know what the other person is going through. Greeting a person with respect, whether we know them or they are a complete stranger to us, won't harm us, but if it helps the other person feel even 1% better, it is worth it, isn't it? A simple hello, a sweet smile, a compliment for no matter how small a thing it may be for, doesn't cost us anything, but the effect it creates in return is just priceless.

Recently, there was something strange that I experienced. Even now, when I think about it, I can't help but laugh at myself but simultaneously, the funny thing is, that the memory doesn't leave me bitter; it actually leaves me feeling a little good about myself(hehe). So, here is what really took place –

...

I was sitting in a metro, headed to meet a friend. I knew my destination but, since I was travelling for the first time there by the metro, I wasn't sure which platform would drop me nearest to my destination. I was confused between 3 stops, and wanting to confirm the same from someone who may know, I looked around.

It was around 7 P.M. in the evening (as I was heading there after my office) and the metro was pretty empty. Among the few people around me, I saw a boy (who must be in his late twenties) looking keenly at me. He had a friendly and pretty face and thankfully, seemed to be someone who may know the answer to my confusion. After debating with myself for some time, whether to ask him or not, I decided to give it a try.

Just as I was about to open my mouth, he spoke up – as if reading my mind, and enquired if everything was fine. I finally blurted what was bothering me and he let out a small chuckle. Looking at my puzzled expression, he explained that he had been observing me for quite some time as I was staring at the map with all the metro stops, that was put up at the metro gates, and he had guess exactly what was bothering me. To my delight, he said that he was also headed that way and he would be happy to guide me to my destination. I heaved a sigh of relief and accepted his offer, without wasting another second.

As we got down the metro, he told me that we would have to walk a little to reach my destination. As, it was a public place, the weather was good and there were a lot of other pedestrians around, I didn't mind it and saw no harm in trusting him. So, we started walking and chatting, getting to know each other a little. He was good looking and witty, so the walk was quite entertaining for me. Soon, we reached a spot where he stopped, and said this was where we would have to part. We were just outside the mall where I was to meet my friend. He said he had to go further ahead and so we bid each other our goodbyes. I thanked him for accompanying me till my destination and for making the little time that we did spend together, worthwhile.

Though, I was a little late at meeting my friend, it was fine as we had enough time, and it being a Friday night, I was in no hurry to head home. We had a great time and once we had finished our dinner, we decided to head back to our respective places.

As, she was also heading back by the metro like me, we started walking towards it together. To my surprise, I found her going towards the opposite direction, compared to the direction I had come from. I thought she must just be confused and told him that the metro was on the other side. She looked puzzled. She then directed my gaze to the flight of stairs that directly connected the metro station to the mall. She asked me why I would even want to walk all the way to the other direction.

I was spellbound for a moment, after which I narrated all that had happened as I was headed to meet her. After I finished narrating my story, she started to laugh at me mercilessly, that how could I be so naive and trust a complete stranger. I tried to defend myself, but it was in vain. Finally, when she was done making fun of me, we got into our respective metros to our way back home.

On the way back as I pondered on the events of the day, I was surprised to find that I didn't feel anger towards the stranger for misguiding me and for making me walk so much unnecessarily. I actually had this little smile on my lips, thinking that he must have found me interesting enough to have wanted to spend some time with me. The thought actually made me blush a little, and to some level, I was actually glad this happened. It gave a little boost to my self-esteem. I had found him good-looking, and seeing that he must have felt the same, oddly felt good. What he did was wrong to some level, but why he must have done that, simply made me feel good. After all, who doesn't like a fan moment!

...

We don't know what others intentions are for doing anything that they do, but, if believing their intentions are for something good gives us happiness, I feel it just makes our life easier. I really don't know what his intentions to lie to me were – it could be that he really didn't know about the direct metro to the mall or could be anything else. Whatever it was, I cannot change that now. So, why not believe that he had a little crush on me and wanted to spend some time with me to get to know me a little, thus making myself feel delighted of the entire episode. This way, whenever I am reminded of that few minutes of my life, I feel happiness within me and I don't feel the need to blame myself for maybe being a little naive.

We should try and simplify our life and try to look at the positive in everything. We know how hard life can be; knowing this, if there is even a tiny bit we may play to make a few seconds of somebody else's life happier, we should grab the opportunity. It may not make much of a difference for us, but we never know how that small act may affect the other person. For that someone, it may be a moment of happiness to cherish forever.

A quote which I really relate to goes as follows:

> *"Sometimes the smallest things take up the most room in our heart."*
>
> – Winnie The Pooh

Photo by Chris Liu on Unsplash

Never Lose Hope

You will reach where you are bound to

When I was little, I used to believe that we all grew up to become actors, and my dream was to grow up to be like my favourite actor of that time. Then slowly, as I grew up, I started to understand that this wasn't the case. So, gradually my dream changed and then I started aiming to be a teacher. As kids we all have dreamt of growing up to be a teacher, haven't we? Everything about being a teacher seemed so fascinating with the little understanding we had back then. I wanted to be a teacher so that even I could write on the black-broad while teaching, give homework to the students and check them the next day. I would also get to scold and punish the ones who hadn't done the given task. I would be able to set the exam paper where I would know all the answers and only I would have the power to mark any answer right or wrong, using the red pen we used to see our teachers use. It surely seemed to be a fun job.

Growing older still, I next started dreaming to be a doctor like my father. It seemed to be such a perfect profession to be in; treating patients and getting them rid of their misery. It seemed like magic. I would admire the respect these patients would shower on my father and now started aiming at being like him when I grew up. However, once I started with my higher secondary, very soon I realised that it wasn't the profession for me. This way my dreams kept changing as I grew up and ultimately, I landed being a Software Engineer by profession (but many things at heart).

When we were young and we would watch these fairy tales, we would be so inspired by the perfect endings. What we failed to take note of is the struggle that goes in between and the hardship required to reach that perfect ending. All the fairy tales shows how difficult the main subject's life is before he/she meets their perfect ending. We dream to be many things, but we are not ready to put in the effort that is required for it. Ultimately if we fail even once, we lose all our hopes and, it being in our human nature, we try to find someone to blame it on, and more often than not, we end up blaming God. We complain how unfair life has been to us and try to make ourselves believe that our bad luck is the cause of our failure and not our lack of dedication for the same.

We hear people say that life isn't a fairy tale, but, I don't quite agree with it. We can make our life similar to that of a fairy tale, if we are ready to put in the hard work that is required to meet our perfect ending. If we are dedicated enough to do that, everybody's life will be like a fairy tale.

As children, most of us must have heard and sung this song – I have a dream, a song to sing by the Swedish pop group ABBA. If we really get into its lyrics, we will observe what a positive message it actually holds within. It says in very simple words to try and find good in everything we see and never be disheartened even if we fail, because when we do believe in ourselves, success will surely follow, no matter how long it takes. If a person understands this truth of life, he has nothing to worry as he has cracked this puzzle we call life. This is why I have always loved and admired this song. When I was a kid, I simply loved it for its tune, but as I grew older and started to understand its actual meaning, it made me love the fact that how easily the lyricist of this song has included the most important secret of how one should lead his/her life.

In life, there are times when we feel that we are good for nothing. We must have really tried to succeed in various fields, but with no luck. Anyone in this situation is bound to lose hope. But, still we must try any hold on to that little ray of hope and try and understand that the reason for our failure is just because we haven't yet been able to figure out where our actual potential lies. We need to believe that it is just not the right time, and things will fall in place when we are actually ready for it. Things just turn out to be better when we least expect it. Till then we need to keep our hopes alive and keep fighting our way through whatever obstacles are placed before us.

I feel having hope is the most important thing in life. After all, whatever we do is actually based on some sort of hope – We work hard in the hope of getting better appraisal, which again is based on the hope of making our present and future more secure; we exercise in the hope of either losing weight or to just be fit so that we may not fall prey to some illness; we try and eat healthy food in the hope of being healthy; we take medicines when we are ill in the hope of getting cured of our illness; and so the list goes on. Without any hope in life, we will just be like a non-living thing. Hope is what keeps us alive and going.

One quote that I truly believe in and which describes the actual meaning of 'Hope' goes as follows:

> *Hope is being able to see that there is a light despite all the darkness.*
>
> – Desmond Tutu

Photo by John Bussell on Unsplash

People Don't Shy From Showing Hate...

Why shy from showing love?

While growing up, I have had a lot of crushes – like seriously, a lot of them! But, I have never let even a single one of them have any hint about it. I may even have gone to the extent of making fun of some(just harmless fun), in front of my friends, only so that nobody would even give a thought to the fact that I may secretly have a crush on the person.

I guess it was just because I was too scared of rejection; we all are, aren't we? So scared was I, that I wouldn't even tell my friends about it, for the fear that it would leak somehow and fall on the person's ear. But however, I wouldn't be scared of the fact that I made fun of the person in front of my friends; even that could reach his ears, right?

When I try to reason this out though, I feel it was because, somehow, I felt that showing my love for the person (who may or may not have felt the same for me), would have portrayed me as weak. However, did making fun of these people with my friends make me look any stronger? And did it really matter? But, in reality, most of us do hide our love, and showing hate feels easy.

How often do we say 'I Love You' to our parents or our siblings? Similarly, once the honeymoon period of a marriage is over, how often do we say 'I Love You' to our spouse? If we think about it, it's not very often, right? Maybe we do say it to our spouse every now and then, but hardly ever to our parents. And giving it a thought, I don't remember saying it directly to my siblings ever!

Now, how often do we fight with them, or stop talking to them to show our anger or hate? There are quite a few instances to think of. And the most number of fights we have all had is with our siblings. We have told our parents, at several occasions that they won't understand what we are going through, or fought with them if any of our wishes isn't fulfilled. Let's not even get into how much we may fight or argue with our spouse.

We know that these people are the most important ones in our lives and we love them dearly, more than life itself, as we may say. We fight and argue with them as we believe we own them and have a right over them. We take them for granted. Same goes for a few of those special friends who are like family to us – sisters/ brothers from another mother. We don't ever shy in showing them our anger. Then why don't we ever show them our love as easily as we show them our hate?

I have noticed many times, that as sweet as I am while talking to strangers, I may lack a lot of that sweetness while interacting with the people who really mean the world to me. The justification that I give myself is that they belong to me. I can be myself with the people I love and I don't need to pretend. But, to think about it, don't the people we love deserve to be shown our love and appreciation? We may show them our hate and anger, for sure; we may speak our mind and open our hearts in front of them, but why not show them our love as well?

We always worry what others will think about us; mind you, these others are always strangers or people who don't really matter to us much. We are on our best behaviour in front of these people. But, does it really matter what these people think about us? It doesn't, as they hardly know the real us. When we aren't concerned with showing our true self to our loved ones, anyone apart from them should be the least of our concerns.

As we proceed in this journey of life, we have heard people say for several people, that they do love you a lot but they don't show. Some may even say that this is his/her way to show that they love or care. Sometimes though, I feel it is necessary to show how much we love the other person, and our love should be clear to the other person. Actions matter I agree, but sometimes, PDAs (public displays of affection) are also necessary. Don't our loved ones deserve to know how much we love them and be pampered by us every now and then?

We express our love when we lose a person; when they won't even get to know about it, but not while they are in our lives. Shouldn't we tell them how fortunate we feel we are, to have them in our lives while they are around, and not wait till it is too late?

When we write a eulogy for a person, it is usually written when the person is no more. We pour our hearts out in it. It is a way to show how amazing the person was and how dearly we will miss them. But do they know how we actually feel for them while they are alive? I feel everyone should know how the other actually feels about them (at-least our close ones). This way we won't have the regret that we didn't let the other person know of our love towards them; we won't have to write in our eulogy that we wish we would have gotten the chance to let the person know while they were with us.

A simple 'Thank You', 'Sorry', 'I Love You' go a long way. We may not see the effect immediately, but it does make a difference in the long run. It makes the other person realise that we do care and appreciate their efforts. Above all, it shows that the person matters to us and we choose them over our own ego. It feels great to know that we are loved. Even we should make sure that the ones we love are well aware of it, and not deprive them of the amazing feeling.

A quote that explains this perfectly goes as follows:

> *Sometimes, love is more important in relationships, but it is not enough... Frequently expressing it is most important to.*
>
> – Pratiksha Ghadge

Competitions Are Good

Only till they are healthy

Photo by Florian Schmetz on Unsplash

When we were in school, we were made to participate in various competitions during our physical activity classes. Even during exams, we were always given ranks based on our performance. Have you ever wondered what the use of those was? They were to help us push ourselves to be the number one; to try to do better every time.

More often than not, while dealing with kids, we always compare them to other kids and get them to obey us by trying to scare them that if they don't, the other kids will get ahead of them, or rather are better than them.

But somewhere, I feel, people forget to teach their kids that it is ok to lose sometimes. They don't have to try and win every race. We are only human. We don't need to be the best in everything. The aim should just be to give in our best, that's it. Everybody can't come first in every race of life. We all are good in something or the other; we can't be good at everything. We just need to find out what that one thing is that we are good at and have interest in, and try to be our best in it.

Winning shouldn't become a habit, because then, when the person feels like he is losing in any race, he falls prey to depression and self-doubt.

People sometimes go overboard while competing with others. I, myself, have come across people who compete with others on everything; it may be good or bad. Competing on positive things still seem to be acceptable to an extent, but competing on the negatives of life, seems just insane. They then come across as emotionless people.

Like if I say, I or any of my known one is suffering from some disease or have fallen prey to some misfortune, they try to compete even in that! They, then tend to narrate instances in which either they or someone dear to them had already faced that exact same disease or misfortune and got it pretty bad. They fail to understand the need to show compassion even at this point, and instead start sharing instances to assure themselves that they aren't lagging behind.

Such people always feel the need to prove that they are better (or have suffered worse) than the other. It is more of rather trying to prove it to themselves, and not the other person. They need to be on the top, they don't care for what it is. It's just what they eventually become. Their sole purpose of life narrows down to putting others down and this makes them feel good about themselves. It is what motivates them.

The purpose of competition should be to better ourselves every day; to try and beat our own best so far. It is to bring out the best in us, help us to utilize our full potential. But we need to try and understand our limit that is the most important part. Competing with others to help us reach our limit is the best kind of competition we may ever have, but once we start overstepping our limit, it is when we actually need to get a hold of ourselves. It is then that we need to understand that we have given our best and be satisfied with it, and if still there are people better than us, then we need to accept it and let it go.

Healthy competition is good, but when a person starts competing in everything with everyone, it slowly consumes the person and they start becoming toxic. They lose any sense of what is right or wrong. They just can't bear to see anyone better than them in anything. This leads to jealousy, and jealousy is good for no one. As they say, excess of anything is bad.

We may have read it or heard it at several occasions, which life is often compared to a race. But I agree to disagree on this logic. I feel life shouldn't be thought of as a race; it just destroys the actual essence of life itself.

It is just life, your life. It should be led at a pace we are comfortable with. Is death any different for a person who has won all the races in life? Is pain or suffering more for the person who hasn't won a single race in his lifetime? No, right? It is the same for every single person.

We just need to aim at doing what gives us satisfaction. When this journey of life is about to end, we should just aim that, when we look back, we don't have anything to regret about, as then it will be too late to rectify anything. Reflecting back on our days that has passed should give us pure happiness and no regrets. It is then that we may say that we have lived life in the best possible way, exactly the way it was meant to be. I feel that should be our sole purpose of life.

One amazing quote I came across that defines healthy competition perfectly, goes as follows:

> *If you continuously compete with others, you become bitter, but if you continuously compete with yourself, you become better.*
>
> – Unknown

Follow Your Heart

To reach great heights in life…

Photo by Chandan Chaurasia on Unsplash

We have always seen in many of the movies and also in real life, that parents always wish for their child to do well in studies so that he/she may get into some good college for either Engineering or Medical. There doesn't seem to be a third career option in their minds. Even we try and follow the path that they try to lay before us, without giving it much thought. It just feels easier maybe, but by the time many of us do realize that it's not where our actual interest lies in, it's too late. By then, we either find ourselves already in one of those colleges, or worse still, in one of those professions. Fearing that turning back now would make people think of us as failures rather than understanding the actual reason, we continue with the path already chosen, till the end of our days. Moreover, it seems as the safest option, doesn't it?

Though the world is progressing drastically and a wide range of career opportunities are opening up, yet Engineering and Medical seems to be the most sought after career options. Any other career option apart from these seems to have a lot of risk involved, and managing to have a successful career in anything apart from these, the possibility seems to be minimal. What people overlook is that Engineering and Medical also have the same percentage of risk involved. Not everyone with an Engineering or Medical degree manages to be successful, and is then made to feel like a failure in life. They are made to believe that they are good for nothing. No consideration is given to the fact that maybe their hearts lie elsewhere and had they been given the chance to follow it, they could also have been successful, and mostly importantly, happy!

It's not that one may never gain success at a profession that they don't enjoy, but they will never feel the satisfaction or any excitement linked to it. A person's success greatly depends on how hardworking and dedicated he/she is, so with these qualities, a person is sure to succeed at any profession they choose. Just imagine the joy they will receive when they succeed at a profession of their liking.

Nowadays, we do see a lot of people choosing various different career options. There are also few brave souls who believe it's never too late to follow your heart and have had the courage to pursue it and actually ace it, setting an example to many. Below I am sharing the life stories of few such people, who have, unknowingly motivated me and left me awestruck by their willpower.

A very close friend of mine did her LLB and further pursued her LLM from a very reputed University in London. After coming back to India, she got a job at a renowned law firm and started her career as an Advocate. She worked for more than a year, and since her qualifications were great, she received good salary from the very beginning itself. But she wasn't happy as she didn't enjoy her work. Finally, after a year and a half, she made the hard decision and quit her well-paying job and decided to do something completely different. At first she started her own venture along with one of her friend, and it did pretty well. Though she liked it, she felt it wasn't good as a long term goal, and she finally switched to digital marketing, and it turned out to be the best decision for her. She has always been good with anything related to creativity and originality, and this helped her soon become popular among her clients. She enjoyed her work and her dedication and hard work helped her grow. She soon reached the height she always aimed for.

Another such example is of a classmate of mine I have always admired. She is blessed with amazingly good looks, is smart and hardworking, and very good in studies. I was sure that she had a bright future ahead. She started her career in Actuarial Science, and according to me, it seemed to be such a perfect career option for her. Few years back I got to know that she had switched her job profile and is now a Makeup Artist (MUA).

Initially I was a little confused as to why had she left her secure job and taken such a risk. There are so many MUA and to make you a known name among them would surely require a lot of time, hard-work and patience. But she was ready for it. Initially she took proper training and certification courses to perfect her in this field. Then, she opened up her own studio, and began marketing her talent through social media channels. Her work just seemed so amazing. I even had the privilege to get decked up by her once and was awestruck by her dedication. She was just perfect at her profession and had an eye for every minute detail. It didn't take her long to make herself a well-known name as a MUA irrespective of the huge competition.

This made me realize that when you enjoy your work, you can overcome the greatest of obstacles. No one can stop you from reaching the height that you deserve and aim for.

Why is it said that we should do what we love? It is because, only when we seriously love what we do, we tend to dedicate ourselves completely into it. We put our heart, mind and soul into it, and thus the outcome we get from it is simply the best we could ever give.

Practically it is not possible for each one of us to give up our secure jobs to follow our hearts, as everything requires time and money. What we can do instead is that, we could start first by actually trying to understand what it that we really enjoy doing is. We may start by dedicating a few hours of our day on it on a daily basis (as consistency is the key), and then slowly mastering it. Then when we are confident enough about our choice, we need to decide on how we want to go ahead with it. We need to keep an open mind for failures and be ready to take the risk that is involved.

One very logical quote that beautifully defines the pleasure, as well as the risk involved when we follow our heart, goes as follows:

> *"Your heart and your instincts are far more reliable than your brain. When you follow your heart, you can be sure you won't regret it later. Even if you calculate your every move, it's not like life ever goes according to plan."*
>
> \- Nithya Menen

Photo by Janko Ferlič on Unsplash

You And I

Separated by distance, not by heart

I felt an instant liking towards her, though I couldn't exactly pinpoint the reason why. Maybe it was because my heart already knew that we were going to be the best of friends, before my mind could even think of it.

It was January of 2015, and it was her wedding. Her name is Maira. She was going to be married to one of my spouse's childhood friend, Abeer, and we all had gathered to be a part of their great day. She was sitting there, so beautiful and yet so simple; I instantly felt a connection with her. Amidst a lot of fun and laughter, the wedding was soon done and we returned back to our respective cities and lives.

After around a year, Abeer's parents shifted to the same city as ours, and so they would visit our city few times in a year, to meet them. During these visits, since they always had a packed schedule, we could hardly ever plan a get-together. On the rare occasions that we did, it would always be just for a short duration. I never actually got a chance to get to know her.

As we were going about our usual lives, we were suddenly hit by the first wave of COVID-19. The entire country was put into a state of lockdown to try and control the outbreak. Still, cases started to rise drastically and there was fear everywhere. All types of commute were completely prohibited. People were stuck away from home for months.

As soon as things began to be little under control, the government allowed inter-state commute in small numbers so that people could go back to their families. By September, Abeer along with his wife, Maira, also managed to come to our city to stay with his parents till this pandemic would hopefully end. Since, everyone was now working from home; he thought it best to spend time with his parents during this difficult phase. Also, the situation at their city was much worse than that in ours, so it was for the best.

Till November of 2020, we didn't even meet them, though we were in the same city and our houses were not even 5km apart, for the fear of infecting each other unknowingly. By that time they even had a baby girl with them who was just around a year old, adding to all the more reason for none of us wanting to take even 1% risk.

Then, as the cases started to subside and were a lot under control, one fine day we planned to meet for dinner. They decided that they would leave their child with his parents and we could have a quick dinner at a nearby place. This place was finalised since it had an open seating and wouldn't be crowded, hence safer. So, finally we 4 did meet and we had a great time together. This time, since it was just the 4 of us and our husbands were busy talking among themselves, we got a chance to interact with each other and it felt so good. We planned to meet again sometime soon, just the two of us.

Soon another month passed, but neither of us could muster the courage to ask the other to meet, as we really didn't know how it would be. The dinner that night had been great and we didn't want to ruin that. Still, finally Maira and I did plan and meet in January over coffee. Once we got to talking, it felt as if we had known each other for years. We poured out our hearts to each other, and then there was no stopping us. We started meeting over for coffee after office hours, whenever possible, and would chat for hours. She even planned a surprise birthday treat for me, a day before my birthday, which was not at all expected, and I was deeply touched by her sweet gesture.

But soon, our country was hit by a second COVID-19 wave, and it was much more severe than the first. This time it felt as if every household had been affected by it. We stopped stepping out of the house completely, not even after the cases had reduced substantially.

Finally, after around 4 months, we did plan and met one another again, and it felt so good. But now, since it was long since they had come over to our city, it was time for them to go back and get back to their normal routine. Abeer's office had also reopened and he was asked to join back at the earliest. Then on, time seemed to move forward in an unimaginable speed, and before I knew it, they were back to their city.

We promised to stay in touch. We both knew that slowly as the days passed by and we got busy with our lives, it wouldn't be possible for us to keep in touch on a regular basis. What we were really sure of was, no matter how often we talked or met, whenever we actually did, it would feel the same. No amount of time would ever be able to diminish our friendship. It's because once your heart connects to another, nothing can ever separate it.

Perfect relationships; be it with our family, friends, lovers or our spouse; are the ones that just clicks naturally and automatically. It's something inside us that just feels right. The bond is not forced or faked. We don't need to put in any extra efforts to maintain it. The thing that matters the most is to just be true and be you, because this relationship is a connection between hearts. It is like being soul mates. Time doesn't matter: you don't need to be friends with someone for years to develop this connection. It is something that just happens, just like that.

A quote which perfectly explains this perfect connection I feel, goes as follows:

> *"A friend is a second self."*
>
> Aristotle

Photo by Kelly Sikkema on Unsplash

Expectations Hurt

Never keep expectations from anyone

Since I was a little kid, my father would always tell me not to keep expectations from anyone, as it will only result to hurt. Back then I used to think that by anyone he must be referring to friends and relatives. My family wasn't just anyone, isn't it? I have a right over them and so having expectations from them, seemed like my birth right. After all they are mine.

While growing up, my family was never into things like surprises. We only wished each other during birthdays and our parent's anniversary. It was an unsaid rule that only the elders would give gifts to the younger ones, and for my siblings and me, elder ones just meant our parents. We kids never exchanged gifts among ourselves and life seemed so easy.

One such year, I recall, my parents had forgotten all about my birthday and I was deeply hurt. I refused to eat dinner and cried myself to sleep. But next day I had forgotten all about it and was back to my jolly self (the joy of being a child).

Now when I sometimes sit and give a thought on that day, my father's words make so much sense. It was such a small and insignificant incident and yet I was so gravely hurt, all because of having expectations. I had expected them to remember my birthday, to wish me and give me gifts. When this didn't happen, I was certain they didn't love me at all.

Had I not have had any expectations; it wouldn't have made any difference. Instead, all the birthdays that they had made so special for me, would have each given me immense joy, as it would all had been a surprise, every single time. Wouldn't that have been much better?

As we grew older, my elder sister was the first one to move out of the city for her higher education. When she first visited us during her summer break, she brought little gifts for my younger brother and me. It was such a pleasant surprise since I had never received any gifts from her. I was so happy with it and kept it preserved for months.

Seeing us so happy with the gifts, she started getting us small gifts every time she visited home during her holidays. This trend was carried on by me when it was my turn to leave the city for my higher education. My bother being the youngest, enjoyed being pampered by both his elder siblings.

Days passed and soon we started working. With our first salaries, we got gifts for our parents. It was the first time in our lives that we had gifted anything to our parents, as it had always been the other way round, and the feeling was so heavenly. We started buying gifts for each other as well, irrespective of age. Slowly we started to look forward to these gifts and would feel bad if the other forgot to get one in any occasion.

During my entire spinster life, though it was 'almost' perfect; with me always having the support of my family for whatever I wished to do, having the best set of friends, loving colleagues, just the best of everything I could have ever expected; still there was always one thing that used to trouble me a lot. It was the fact that I had never received any proposals from any boy, while I would see all my friends receive several. I used to have so many crushes, but I always expected them to approach me first, which resulted in me losing any little chance I had.

This sorrow, as it did felt back then, seems so minuscule now. It was just my expectations that were causing me this sorrow. Why did I have this expectation from them to come and propose to me first, when I could also have done the same, but I didn't? Had I not had this unjustified expectation, my life would have felt perfect to me as well, and I would have enjoyed it to the fullest, not having this lingering thought to bother me at the back of my mind.

Since the time I have been married, I have always tried to plan something exclusive for my husband for his birthdays, as I feel the more time and effort I put in planning and implementing it, will symbolize how much he matters to me and my love for him. Since time is the most important thing one can give the other in the present world, amidst our busy schedules, this is the way I feel is perfect to show my love for him. When I don't see him reciprocating the same for my birthdays, I feel hurt.

When I contemplate on this later, I feel what I need to make myself understand is, that this is just my belief; it doesn't need to be right or everyone needn't be of the same opinion. I shouldn't expect this from him as well. He is an individual person with his own beliefs. His way of showing his love will obviously be different from mine. Only because it's different from mine, doesn't mean that he loves me any less. So, it's meaningless for me to lose my peace over it.

If we try and reflect at all those times that we felt hurt or sad, we will notice that the cause of all these sufferings, the cause of our unhappiness, has always been expectations. We tend to have expectations from so many people, situations and things. We even have expectations from strangers for that matter. Let's take a simple example: while driving our car, we expect the others to drive properly and follow all the rules, and when they don't, we feel anger.

Why do we have such expectations? Wouldn't it be better if we drive our car, minding our own business, not allowing a moment of distraction and having full concentration on the road? This way, I feel, even the number of accidents would decrease drastically and we will become better drivers.

I understand that having completely no expectations is easier said than done, and is, in a way, impossible. But at least we can try training our minds to have fewer expectations. Once we have been hurt, we should try and learn from our mistakes and try not to have the same expectations again. This will ultimately help us in leading a better and happier life.

Not having expectations will also help us to look at the beauty of things, love everyone and everything for the way it is. This world itself will seem much more beautiful than what it already is. Life will be treasured and cherished. Life won't be a burden for anyone anymore and everyday will seem like a gift from the Almighty.

One such quote, depicting the beauty of not having expectations that is really close to my heart goes as follows:

> *My expectations were reduced to zero when I was 21. Everything since then has been a bonus.*
>
> \- Stephen W. Hawking

Life Goes On...

Life doesn't stop for anyone

Photo by Michael Skok on Unsplash

When I was in school, I had a best friend. She used to understand me like no one else was ever able to. I never thought I could find any other friend like her. She meant so much to me that I felt life would be impossible without her.

Then I grew a little older and started going to college in a new city. Initially there wasn't a single moment that I didn't miss my parents or my best friend from school. Then, as the days passed, I started making friends in college and days started getting better. Some became really good friends. I still used to miss my parents and my school's best friend, but the frequency became little less and life started feeling less miserable without them.

Soon I adjusted completely well in my college life and started enjoying my days, when I grew older further, and soon it was time to leave college and start the next phase of my life – my professional life. I had got into one of the best companies through college placement and would soon be joining it.

I again felt my life falling apart and dreaded to even think how I would even survive without my college beasties by my side. I was sure I was never going to find such friends at my work place. After all it's said once you start working, everyone is your colleague but none are your friend.

Still, as life is, I moved on leaving my beautiful school and college days and friends behind. As more such days passed by, I found myself actually starting to enjoy this new phase of my life, and astonishingly, I had managed to make some good friends here as well. And when I say friends, I mean real friends and not just colleagues. I started to enjoy life once again.

But just then, once again, life happened. As always, just when I was again enjoying and loving life, I grew older still, and now I was to move to yet another phase of my life – my married life. I was to get married and move to yet another completely new city. This time I was certain that my fun days were behind me, and now it would all be about relationships and responsibilities.

But thankfully, I was again proved to be wrong. I soon settled on to this new phase of my life, which though was so different from the life I have had so far, yet had its own charm. I now have a husband, who is always by my side, like a forever friend, and I again managed to make new good friends at my new work place, and of course, my husband's friends who soon became my friends, the best friends' type.

I still miss my school, college and office friends and talk to them occasionally. Whenever I get a chance to meet them, it's always like those good old days and we have a gala time. But life didn't stop for any of us. We all have moved on with our lives and gotten busy in it.

Life goes on, it never stops. Many times in our life, we feel this is the end, or that we are never going to overcome a particular situation, but that's not the case. We move on, leaving precious memories along the way. We never forget the ones who touched our lives, but we all do get busy in our current lives. Occasionally, when we do take a peek back, we may find a small smile playing on our lips, and we may also shed a silent tear or two, as we revisit the good old days and miss our dear friends, but life goes on.

As Dr. Seuss rightly said:

"Don't cry because it's over, smile because it happened."

– Dr. Seuss

In the end we realize, the only person who is always going to be with you is you. Only you are permanent in your life, everybody else is temporary.

People are meant to come and go, helping us walk on this path of life. People come into our lives, and leave once there part in our life is done, leaving behind just memories. In the end, it is just us, alone with all these precious memories.

This quote by Lao Tzu, I feel, describes life perfectly:

> *"New beginnings are often disguised as painful endings."*
>
> — Lao Tzu

Never Take Your Blessings For Granted

Sometimes we only realize it when it is gone

Photo by Carolyn V on Unsplash

What do we count as a blessing? When we think about it, we usually count on things like having a good family, a decent and well-paying job, a beautiful home to live in, good friends, never to have to stay hungry, getting good education and the list goes on.

But have you ever thought about the little things in life, that is also a form of blessing? Little things like being able to sleep at night, waking up in the morning, being able to see the beautiful nature we are surrounded with, being able to eat with our own hands, being able to walk around all by ourselves, such everyday things that we take for granted so easily. We don't ever consider these as a blessing, it's like it is a part of life. Does everybody in this world have these blessings that we overlook every day? Do we ever thank God for these blessings? And if you think about it, these are the greatest blessings among all other things which we actually consider as a blessing. These are the things that actually matters the most in life.

Imagine having to live without even 1 of these blessings, which we sort of consider to be our birth right, being born as a human. These are the blessings we should value the most in life, without which, none of the things that we usually count as blessings, would mean the same ever.

I realized this recently when I became deprived of one such blessing (which till now I had never ever realized to be such a great blessing and that I was the luckiest to have been granted it), i.e. being able to sleep at night. Yes, this may sound so inconsequential as compared to any other much-needed blessings, like having good eyesight, hands and legs, good health, as I had mentioned earlier, but believe me, sleep is as important a blessing as any other.

I was always the one who was considered to be able to sleep anywhere and at any time. Nothing could prevent me from falling asleep, be it people talking around me, television blaring, and music being played in full volume, all the lights on, be it a moving car or a plane, just nothing. It was so obvious, that all my friends and family members often used to joke about it.

It was to such an extent that even during night-outs with my girlfriends, after all the partying, as we would sit down and start chit-chatting among ourselves till late at night (thing that we girls love the most), I would be the only one dozing off sitting right there in the middle of the group.

Sometimes it would also lead me to embarrassing situations when I would fall asleep in-between of a family gathering, or worst of all, between boring office meetings. My friends in office would often make videos of me dozing off sitting at my seat, and would use it to embarrass me later at several occasions (yes, we all know that's what friends are good at ;) They love you, care for you, but wouldn't miss the slightest opportunity to embarrass you).

I would listen to so many people complain about not being able to sleep; some would require complete silence, some required the room to be completely dark to be able to sleep. I have even know few people who could only get sleep on their usual bed, any change in location or bed would result to them not being able to get sleep at all. It was always little difficult for me to understand how these things could deprive a person of sleep. Sleep, according to me, seemed to be something so easy; it didn't require any effort at all. It would just come so naturally to me. I would boast about it to the whole world, until the day I faced it the very first time.

It started around a year back. It had been a day like any other, with me getting up in the morning, getting ready for my work, spending the usual 9 hours working at office, then coming back home, eating, watching some television and finally retiring for the day. But this night was different. I had been lying awake in my bed for a long time waiting to fall asleep, but I just couldn't. I tried everything I had heard of, which usually would help one in falling asleep; things like counting 1 to 100 and then back in the reverse order in my mind, focusing on the circular movement of the ceiling fan, taking deep breaths to calm my mind, but nothing seemed to help at all. I couldn't believe it at first that this was actually happening to me. I had been lying for hours now with my eyes closed, but I just couldn't fall asleep. The night seemed to be never-ending. Finally, after what seemed like ages, it was dawn. Being tired of lying awake for so long, I finally gave up on sleep and started my day early.

Having office throughout the day I didn't have any time to sleep during the day, but in a way I thought that would be helpful as then I was sure to fall asleep real quickly at night, since I would be so sleep deprived by then. But God had other plans for me. It was the same nightmare for the next 2-3 nights. I had hardly been able to catch a maximum of 2-3 hours of sleep in total, in almost 3 days in a row now. I was mentally and physically exhausted. I couldn't concentrate on anything due to lack of sleep and it started taking a toll on my health. I started getting scared of night, thinking of how I was going to pass the entire night yet again.

Finally, on the fourth day I consulted a Psychiatrist who prescribed me sleeping pills for a few days. I had never thought that I would ever require sleeping pills to fall asleep. I was taken aback. It was then that I realized how great a blessing it was that I had, but I never had considered it to be a blessing, till I became deprived of it.

I had to take those sleeping pills for quite a few months till it was gradually reduced and finally stopped altogether. But, things are not the same anymore. Every night whenever I lie in bed, the first thought that enters my mind is will I get sleep today. Every night I hope to be able to sleep and only get up directly in the morning. Every morning, whenever on those few occasions now, that I do get a sound sleep the entire night, I automatically tend to thank God for it. Such days, now seems like the greatest blessing of all.

So count on all your blessings that God has so gratefully granted you, no matter how small it may seem now, because once you lose it, it is then that we tend to realize the actual worth of it.

As rightly quoted by Woodrow Kroll:

> *"Concentrate on counting your blessings and you'll have little time to count anything else."*

Photo by Anusha Hansaria

Life At A Jungle

Is our life tougher?

It was just a while back that I finally got an opportunity to visit one of the places I had been wanting to visit since a long time now - the Ranthambore National Park, which is situated in Rajasthan, India. It is famous for its tigers and is one of the best locations in India to see the tigers in its natural habitat.

Here they have divided the entire jungle into zones and some of these zones are open for tourists to witness the actual life at a jungle, without any human intervention. The forest authorities have fixed slots for safaris, in which tourists may visit the jungle and that too only in registered vehicles with registered drivers. They don't allow private vehicles inside the jungle premises. This is done to protect the animals from any poachers and to minimise human intervention into their natural habitat as far as possible.

The general public need to pre-book the safari slots, and in a single trip, a single zone is covered and its duration is 3 hours. However, government vehicles have access to all the zones (the ones which are open for safaris) and they may switch between zones in a single safari.

Since Ranthambore is just 8 hours' drive from the place where I live, we decided for a road trip. By the time we reached Ranthambore, it was evening and we were exhausted. We had an early dinner and retired for the day, as we had a safari booked for early morning the next day. This being my first open jeep safari I was extremely excited and found myself lying awake the entire night.

Soon it was morning and we all got ready and mounted the jeep, ready for the safari to begin. Once we entered the jungle premises, we were advised not to make any noise as it would disturb the animals. So we sat silently with our cameras ready, to capture all the glimpse of forest life that we could witness.

At this point, I should say that these jeep drivers are very well trained and experienced. Our jeep driver kept telling us all about the history of the jungle as he drove through the zone, but simultaneously he was fully alert of any unusual movement or warning cry that the animals would make. Whenever he would feel he heard the cry of any animal, he would stop the jeep and ask us to silently observe. This would happen at multiple occasions.

One thing that I observed at these occasions was that, the less powerful animals like the Deers and Sambars(a large deer native to the Indian subcontinent, South China and Southeast Asia), seemed to live under constant fear of being attacked by the mighty predators. Deers and Sambars usually roam in herds. If any of them feel or smell danger, they give out a peculiar cry to warn the others of potential danger. At even the faintest of sounds, they would stop grazing and become alert of any movement in the bushes or in their surroundings, ready to run for their lives.

These animals seemed to live in constant fear of their lives. They need to be aware of their surroundings at every point of time as there may be a predator lurking around anywhere and anytime. They can't even sleep peacefully at night. They can't leave a moment unguarded.

This got me thinking of how fortunate we are. We live at the comfort of our homes with all the possible securities taken care of. We have the army protecting us from the terrorists, the police protecting us from criminals, the doctors curing us of any diseases, and the list goes on. But who do these animals have to save them and help them to get rid of their sufferings?

Most of the times we know we are safe. Yet, majority of the humans suffer from depression, anxiety and insomnia (to state the least minimum). Nobody is happy or satisfied with the life they have. We always want more and keep complaining about every single thing. We have forgotten to count our blessings. Human nature is such that we only focus on the negative, which may just be really minute if compared to all the blessings that have been showered upon us.

We all need to stop for once, and try to focus on how blessed our life is, in comparison to so many less fortunate than us. Focus on what we have rather than what we don't. Wouldn't life become boring if there was nothing our heart could desire for? Would there be any purpose to live then?

Life is beautiful because of the way it is. Had it been any different, it wouldn't be worth living for.

A beautiful quote about life I came across goes as follows:

> *Life was meant to be lived, and curiosity must be kept alive. One must never, for whatever reason, turn his back on life."*
>
> — Eleanor Roosevelt

Photo by Sarah Kilian on Unsplash

Is This The New Normal?

Will our lives remain like this forever?

New Year's Eve was as great as ever, with all of us excited to welcome the upcoming year with open arms. For most of us, the year started on a good note. For me it was extra special since I had landed a job at my dream company, the very first month of the year itself.

The first two months went by without any indication about what the rest of the year may carry. If we had any hint about what was to follow back then, thinking about it now, I feel I would have wanted to do several things differently. But that isn't the way life is, is it?

The month of March started, and slowly we started hearing about this new virus named COVID-19. The number of cases reported was few, but nonetheless, it created havoc amongst people. By the mid of March, most of the companies started shutting down and employees were told to work from home (WFH). Within days, the entire state was put into strict lockdown with night curfew in place. Every mode of public transport and all the public gathering places were closed. People who were found stepping out of their homes without any valid urgency were punished by the police.

Even at that time, everyone thought it to be a temporary phase which would soon pass. But, as the lockdown period kept increasing, the gravity of the situation started getting clear. The number of COVID-19 cases started increasing drastically. People started to lose their jobs due to financial crisis, migrant worker were stranded with no money, no job and no means to go back to their homes, students were stuck in hostels and there was chaos everywhere.

With ever increasing COVID-19 cases even with all these restrictions implemented, it slowly became difficult to keep the state in complete lockdown for any longer. So gradually lockdown started to be lifted. Migrant workers and students were sent back to their homes as the first step. Soon, the lockdown was completely lifted, except for few limitations.

People say we need to learn to live with COVID-19, they say it is the new normal. But somehow, I agree to disagree with this. I refuse to accept this will be our life henceforth.

In 1918, when the world was infected with Spanish Flu, it must have seemed the way it does now. But, didn't the world overcome it? Our lives were normal before being stuck with COVID-19, so why won't it be after it. Today, as compared to 1918, the world has made great advances in the field of medicine, and we are bound to find a cure to this pandemic much faster than that of 1918 pandemic.

Surely, it will take time for the world to heal back to normal, but it will and we will get our normal lives back. I don't mean we shouldn't bother about COVID-19, but instead, we should all stick as one to overcome this pandemic sooner. We should take all the necessary precautions to be safe and keep others safe. We should keep on our fight against this pandemic for as long as it takes, and believe that our normal life lies just around the corner.

We all need to be strong and have patience. Even after this pandemic is under control, the world will take time to regain back to normalcy.

Meanwhile, what we can do is, keep helping one another in every way possible and not lose hope. There does await a bright day at the end of this dark phase. We just need to hold on tight till we get there.

> *"Hope begins in the dark. The stubborn hope that if you just show up and try to do the right thing, the dawn will come. You wait and watch and work: you don't give up." – Anne Lamott, Novelist*

Photo by Gabriele Diwald on Unsplash

The Unseasoned Rain

It was a hot summer afternoon. The sun was blaring in its full brightness. Nothing was helping to soothe the heat. Even the water from the tap was boiling, so you can imagine how hot a day it was.

I was sitting by the window, biting on some ice-cubes to cool myself and praying to the Gods for some rain to relieve us of this heat. Just then, as in response to my prayers, suddenly the sky was covered with dark grey clouds. Within minutes, the day turned dull and soon I could see huge droplets of water pouring from the heavens above.

It wasn't the rainy season, so it came as a surprise, but the most pleasant one, to all of us. But it wasn't just water droplets that poured, along came the hailstorm. We could see it hitting the roads and the cars parked on it. Little kids rushed to their balconies with mugs to collect these chunks of ice. The excitement on their faces was priceless. They would collect some and put it in their mouths. It was such an amazing sight.

Soon the hailstorm stopped but the rain continued. We all rushed outdoors to welcome it with open arms. Soon the roads were full of people dancing in the rain and enjoying the relief from the heat it offered. The rain Gods seem to be enjoying the sight and let the rain continue for another few hours.

Slowly people started heading back to their homes to dry themselves and indulge in some hot and delicious snacks accompanied by tea. I got back to my home as well, and after changing to some dried cloths, I again went and sat at my favourite spot near the window, admiring the rain and how all the trees, that looked dead by the blazing heat of the sun, now seemed so lush green and full of life in the rain.

Finally, it stopped raining, but the clouds still lured over, preventing the Sun from shining, the rest of the day.

This rainy day, in middle of the summer season, made me contemplate how much a break from a routine is appreciated. Do we enjoy rain so much during the rainy season as much as we enjoyed it in middle of the summer season?

Getting ready to go to school and then suddenly getting to know that school is closed for some particular reason made us feel like the happiest person in the world when we were little, summer and winter breaks compared nothing in front of these surprise holidays.

A surprise visit by a loved one, a surprise gift from someone unexpected, an unexpected promotion at the workplace, finding two toffees inside a single wrapper, a short trip to someplace beautiful, having your favourite dish once in a while, aren't these the most beautiful and cherished memories? Would it be as pleasant if it happens every day? Would partying with friends be as much fun if done every single day? We all know the answer.

A break from the routine is always welcomed as it refreshes us and provides us the strength to go on with our life. It's just small bonus from life, a feel-good factor. It helps keep us motivated and helps us to appreciate life.

For that matter, every type of surprises are important, be it the pleasant or the unpleasant ones. Having the unpleasant ones makes us really appreciate the pleasant ones. Having the bad ones, makes us realise the worth of good. No surprise is worthless.

This reminds me of a quote by Boris Pasternak, which reads as

Surprise is the greatest gift which life can grant us.

Photo by Steve Halama on Unsplash

All I Ever Wanted Was Love!!!

Why is it so hard to find love in this world?

Since the time I was a little girl, all I ever wanted was to be loved, to be accepted the way I was. Was it too much to ask?

As I lay wide awake on my bed in the middle of the night, I try to rewind my entire life in front of my eyes to try and figure out where did I actually go wrong? I rewind it again and again, but to no avail. I am still unsure as to which major part did I actually miss.

I have always been a romantic at heart and would always dream of a fairy-tale type of life, where no matter who you are or where you are, your Prince Charming would always find you, where the entire universe gets together to make you meet your lover, where you are the most loved character among all. I have always dreamt of such type of life. But we all know dreams are just meant to be dreamt of, it doesn't ever come true. That's the difference between a dream and reality.

I have always been on the weaker side, health-wise, since the time I was a little girl. Due to which, my elder sister would always be the one my aunt would want to take to the market rather than taking me and risking me falling. I would always feel left-out and disheartened. She, being an extrovert, people seems to like her more and I grew up always wanting to gain the attention my sister would get.

In my school days, I was a very introvert girl and wouldn't talk much. I always felt no one loved me and would make fun of whatever I uttered, so preferred to keep my mouth shut. I was average at studies which contributed further to make me feel dumb in front of my classmates. I had accepted love wasn't for me and the last thing I wanted was my classmates laughing at me. School soon got over, and unlike others, I was happy about it.

Soon I got into college and decided to focus on my studies. I thought maybe if I do well in studies, people would automatically love me, as I had always seen in school that toppers were always the most loved ones. I made friends in college, good ones, and was happy for once. My grades did improve drastically and more and more of my batch mates started to interact with me. It felt like a good phase. But, this was also the phase of our lives where we craved for the attention of the opposite sex. I would see all my girlfriends falling in love and getting so many proposals. Me on the other hand, any guy would just approach me to either ask for my notes or to ask some doubt related to some subject. Before any exams I was the one to get the most number of calls, but all asking for some or the other doubts. Never once did anyone propose me or seem to have a crush on me. Still life went on. Soon college came to an end and this time I was very sad at being parted from my dear friends.

So starts the next phase of my life – Work life, the life as a professional. I got job in a great company and made good friends on the first day itself. Even work was going good, my teammates, my manager, all were happy with my work. Seems like everything is perfect, but what was still missing was love. I had still not seen any guy getting attracted to me or even trying to flirt with me, while all my friends would get so much attention from guys. I failed to understand what it that attracts a guy to a girl was, what it that I was missing was.

Every guy considered me to be a good friend, but things came to a stop there. People around me seem to like me a lot and even enjoyed my company. I, being of a chirpy nature in front of people I am comfortable with, guys used to love pulling my leg and joking with me, but no one ever seem to have a crush on me. I, on the other hand, seem to get crush on every third guy I met, which made it further difficult.

I don't know if it was my fault that I couldn't understand their feelings or if I was very casual at displaying my feelings, but the reason for it was that I was always very scared to let anyone know if I even had a crush on them, as I didn't want to face rejection. More than rejection, it was the fear to be laughed at, to be insulted at how I could even think of it. Maybe they were out of my league. They were bound to get someone better than me, right? And as I had always been influenced a lot by movies and fairy tales, where it is always the guys who take the initial step, I expected the same and kept waiting and hoping.

Slowly days changed to years, and soon my marriage was fixed. In just a gap of 2 months from the day of my marriage getting fixed, I found myself taking the 7 vows of a lifetime of togetherness. Just in the blink of an eye I was married.

My life changed overnight, nothing remained the same. I was happy to be someone's wife, as the way my life had been excluded of love; I highly doubted if anyone would ever want to marry me. Yet, here he was, full of love and care for me.

As the days started to pass, I was again starting to get haunted by my luck with love, as it had been so far. Though my husband is the best thing that ever happened to me, the truth remained the same. He loved me, cared for me, but it felt similar to the way you would love or care for a friend or a sibling. He didn't seem to be attracted to me or love me in a way lovers do. I felt more like a best friend of his than a wife. Though in a way it's the best kind of relation, still I miss what has always been missing in my life, love.

I miss experiencing how it feels when someone is madly in love with you, when someone admires you.

I guess this is life. Everyone has to make sacrifices and I guess this is the sacrifice God wants from me. And, life still goes on. Slowly we learn to live with it. I hope I learn to live with it too. Sometime soon, before the pain gets too much to bear.

New Beginning

This is not the end of the world.

Photo by Jan Tinneberg on Unsplash

It's 10 o'clock in the morning and I am still lying on my bed staring at the ceiling. I don't wish to get up to welcome the new day. It is going to be the same, as the past few weeks have been. We had nothing else to do, apart from being locked indoors. The day seems so long since there isn't much option to entertain one within the constraints of our homes.

Reluctantly, I get up from my bed as lying for so long has given me a backache. I try to not look at the News app notification because the rate by which COVID-19 seem to be increasing is dreadful. I no longer wish to know how many new confirmed cases have come into existence or how many of them have lost their lives to this deadly virus. It seems never-ending, and the rate by which it seems to spread, end of COVID-19 doesn't seem to be near.

The things I used to hate (like going to office on a Monday), now seems to be a desire. As the days are passing, I am starting to crave for these things more. Things like going to office, going to the market (be it just for grocery shopping), going for a stroll at the park, and so many things just related to stepping out of the house. Why is it that when we are restricted to do something, we want to do it more?

Sometimes I wonder what worse than this could happen to me, but immediately I am stuck by the plight of the poor, mainly the daily wagers. As the country is in complete shutdown, we are still sitting at the comforts of our homes, with more than enough food to fill our stomachs, yet we are still complaining. If we think about the daily wagers, think about the life they must be leading with no sufficient money to even feed themselves and their family two times a day, the doctors who risk their lives and the lives of their family members just to help and cure the ones already infected by this virus, the police who are out on the streets so that we stay indoors, the grocery shop owners who open their shops just to provide us the essential food items so that we may not starve, and so many other such people who are out of the comfort of their homes just to provide a comfortable stay for us. Should we let their sacrifice go waste by giving up? It doesn't sound right, does it?

What we can do instead is have faith in the Almighty and look at the positive. Look up at the sky; doesn't it seem clearer and blue? These days we can even catch glimpse of a star studded sky at night. The air quality has improved drastically with no vehicles on the road and the sea has become cleaner. This time has, in fact, given a chance to Mother Earth to replenish itself once again.

Scientist all over the world is trying their best to find a vaccine against this virus, and they are bound to find one soon. In a few days, when this virus is under control, we will have a cleaner and healthier environment to ourselves. This time is temporary, but the positive changes that it will bring will be there for a long time. It will be a new beginning to a pollution free environment, which was not possible otherwise.

This has been correctly quoted in the below lines:

> *"New beginnings are often disguised as painful endings."*
>
> Lao Tzu

So, we may be going through a very tough time as of now, but this is bound to end soon, giving way to a new beginning. So, hold on to your faith a little longer, and this shall soon pass. Till then, stay safe stay home.

Photo by Christina at wocintechchat.com

How I Landed At My Dream Company!!!

Was it mere luck?

We meet people working at big companies, big brands, and all I remember thinking is that they are so lucky to be working at such good organizations. But tell me one thing, is it mere luck that some people get the opportunity to work with such companies while the others don't?

Few months back I got tired of working at a company, and, wanting a break from the redundant life, I resigned, without even having another job in my hands. For around a month I completely relaxed and roamed few of the places I hadn't got time to visit. I was sure that I would get another job whenever I would start looking for it, hence didn't give it another thought. Little did I know I was in for a big shock!

After my break, I started looking for a job without even giving myself some time to prepare for the same. As a result, in the first few interviews, I failed miserably. I would find it hard even to clear the first round. It was devastating, but thankfully I didn't lose hope, not yet.

As they say everything happens for a reason: as I attended more and more interviews, I got a knack of the type of questions that were asked. I started preparing myself accordingly and slowly, but steadily, my interview experience started to improve. Gradually I started to clear the 1st round and in some cases even the 2nd. I started to regain my confidence and feel positive of landing a job soon.

On one such interview, I happened to clear all the rounds. While I waited for the final HR round, I felt pretty sure that this was my breakthrough that I had been waiting for so long, and started dreaming about how my life would change when I start working there. Soon, they called me for the HR round. It was this time that I faced an unexpected rejection. The reason was they were not ready to pay me my expected salary and would therefore not consider my candidature. I was heartbroken. It had taken me nearly a month to prepare myself to this extent that I was able to clear an interview, and still I was rejected.

Then following this, I gave several other interviews and faced similar fate in all. I was clueless. To be unable to clear an interview would be my fault, but to clear and still be rejected was something that was not in my hands. There were so many competitors; companies would always get another candidate whose expected salary would be lesser.

I finally started to lose my confidence and patience. I started to skip interviews thinking what was the used when they would simply reject me even if I would clear all the rounds.

Then someone told me this marvellous law of life:

> *Nothing has ever been achieved before the right time and more than one's luck*

So, I decided not to give up. My time was bound to come, all I needed was persistence. So, I started attending interviews again and performed to the best of my capabilities.

Finally, after a few more weeks of hard work, I did land a job at my dream company. I had finally found the secret to success. It is not just luck or hard work; it is a combination of some luck, hard work, confidence in oneself, and above all, persistence.

Someone rightly quoted this simple rule to success:

"Try try until you succeed."

Photo by Unknown on Unsplash

Is It Wrong To Cry At Your Work-Place?

Does it show your weakness?

Have you every cried at your work-place? Been in that state when you no longer can hold back your tears? Well, I have. Does this mean that I am weak? No, it doesn't.

We all are facing a battle that the other is unaware of, be it in our personal lives or our professional lives. With all the emerging technologies to make our life simple, all we get is a more complicated one.

While these technologies have reduced manual labour to a significant amount, the mental labour has increased drastically. People don't have time for each other. People are glued to their systems or phones. Even if we are sitting in the same room, each one of us is in our own different worlds. Simple conversations have become very rare. Technologies these days, on one hand, allows us to work or connect with the entire world from the comfort of our rooms, while these same technologies, on the other hand, have taken away the personal life of people. People have thousands of friends on social media, but not a single true friend to talk to. When we talk to someone, it relieves us of a lot of stress, but in today's busy world, no one has the time to sit and talk. All are running a race they themselves are unaware of.

On the professional front, as more and more tasks are getting automated, the competition for job, to be able to provide for a better life, to meet the ever increasing demands, is increasing drastically. Everyone is expected to better themselves by every passing day, give in better than that of yesterday. There is another person ready to take your spot always, so people live in constant fear of losing their job, of not being able to meet the ever-increasing needs, constant stress.

This results in every person compromising on their personal life, on their own physical and mental health. People are expected to work like robots. Their work-life balance goes for a toss. People are loaded with more work than they can handle, and in order to fulfil it, life itself is compromised.

How long can a person survive in such condition? Isn't it normal for a person to break down at some point in time? When this point arrives, since most of our time is spent at our work place, is it really such a big deal if this point arrives while we are at our work place and we can just not hold it any longer?

As we already know, crying helps us release a lot of stress and hence make us feel calmer. Once we are out with it, it also helps us to concentrate on our work better. So, in a way it has its own benefits. Also, it is normal to cry as it is an emotion we were born with. Saying this, I don't mean that it is fine to cry like babies for every little thing, but crying once in a while, when you are way too stressed out, is of no harm.

The happy faces we see everywhere doesn't really mean that the person has no sorrow in their life. It simply shows how well the person is able to cope up with their sorrows. But it's not necessary to have that smile on even when you are dying inside. It's ok to give in to your emotions, to express your sorrows. We are human beings after all. Whom are we pretending in front of?

This is very well quoted by Ron Steer in the below quote:

> *"Tears are part of life and express our emotions, sadness and joy. I tell young lads it's OK to cry. Remember that sometimes we need help to pick ourselves up and get our fight back. Never look down on a man that cries, he's being honest."*

Photo by Kristopher Roller on Unsplash

Life... The Way It Is!!!

Why can't life be the way we want it to be?

What is the most appropriate term we may use to describe life? The one that pops up in our minds is – Unpredictable. This is exactly how life is. It is like a thriller movie, where, no matter how hard we try, we can never guess what is to happen next. It is always full of surprises: while some are pleasant, the others may be like a nightmare. It always keeps us on our edge.

Most of the times we feel life is very unfair and unbalanced. When we are undergoing some hard phase in life, all life surrounds us with is more pain and sufferings. It hardly gives us time to come out of one hardship before it drowns us in another, and then another, to the time that we are just on the verge of giving up. Then it turns our clock and surrounds us with so much happiness, which again becomes hard to handle.

People say that it's necessary because it makes us strong and gives us the strength to face it the next time. But, why can't life be balanced? Like, let us overcome one low phases followed by a high phase. Won't life be easier to deal with this way?

But, we don't have a say in how life should be, do we? So, each one of us are compelled to finish this journey called life, the way it is.

Think of it as finding ourselves in the middle of a long tunnel, with neither of its ends in sight. What option do we have then? Its either to keep walking, knowing that there is bound to be a way out, no matter how long the walk is, or giving up and letting ourselves rot in that tunnel itself. The choice is ours.

So, life isn't simple. It requires a great degree of effort to survive through it. But once we near the climax, just like that of a thriller movie, we then realise that all the troubles was worth it.

If we have a mixture of food consisting of sweet and sour, we will enjoy it, no matter what. But imagine eating something bitter followed by something sweet. The sweetness in the second case will be much more welcomed and appreciated. That's how life is. It makes our journey so difficult, that once we overcome it, we may feel the real happiness even in the simplest of things. The things we may not have valued otherwise.

So, it's no use complaining about life and it's ways because it's not in our hands to change it. What we may do instead is to accept it the way it is and have the confidence that we have the strength and motivation to reach the end of that tunnel. We need to believe in ourselves to have the strength to fight whatever life throws towards us and not be a loser. After all who likes to miss the climax?

One of the best sayings about life:

> *Many of life's failures are experienced by people who did not realize how close they were to success when they gave up.*

– By Thomas Edison

What Is Depression?

Are you suffering from depression??

Photo by Cherry Laithang on Unsplash

A lot of people ask me what actually is depression. Everyone has heard about depression, but most people don't know which traits or characteristics are defined as the symptoms of depression. Even at this generation, most people are either not aware of, or are not ready to accept that they have depression and get some medical help, which is very much required.

Depression is not a disease we should be ashamed of: it is a state of mind. In today's world, with the lifestyle we follow, results in 90% of the people suffering from depression. Our lives have become so hectic, which leaves no time for us. We are living a monotonous life with no time to do the things that we love or that make us happy. With increase in the cost of living, everybody is busy trying to earn more and more money, resulting in spending most of our waking hours at our work place. Following ones passion is not considered a priority as it doesn't always help to meet the cost of our living. We don't even have time for our loved ones.

How to know if you have depression, or, in better words, when should you seek medical help?

There are times when we feel low as a result of some loss or some event that didn't execute as per our expectations. This is quite normal and won't be considered as a sign of depression. People with depression often feel extreme sadness or over-joyful for no reason in particular. These are known as mood swings. These mood swings are not in a person's control. During their low phases, they tend to feel everything is against their will, and based on the level of depression one is suffering from, they may get suicidal thoughts. If not controlled at the right time, these thoughts get so severe, that the person may tend to harm itself.

Depressed people tend to get irritated in every small thing. It gets difficult for them to control their anger and may thus seem rude and drive people away from them. In this process, they may spoil their relationship with those who they care for.

People in depression also tend to feel very tired and sleepy all the time, as there is so much going on in their minds, that they are always exhausted mentally. They tend to sleep a lot because firstly, they are tired throughout the day, and secondly, because it helps them to pass their time. This is because when we are sleeping, for that moment the mind is free of thoughts and thus it relaxes us. They just want to get over with their days as quickly as possible. They hate their lives and just live it for the heck of it.

Life seems worthless to these people. They are so full of self-loathing and hatred, that they cannot see the good in anything. They tend to see only the bad in every situation. They feel everyone and everything is against them, that no one loves them. But, this isn't something they do on purpose. When in depression, the mind tends to behave weirdly, in ways that cannot be justified to a normal person.

With depression comes anxiety, which results in lack of sleep, irritability and restlessness. Medications just help to calm the mind and relax the person. It doesn't cure depression, but just relaxes the brain for a certain number of hours, and prevents the person from thinking too much.

Ways to fight depression:

The easiest way to fight depression is by consulting a psychiatrist and following the medications provided religiously. However, the better way to fight depression is, by attending various counselling sessions, exercising and meditation. Being around your loved ones also helps one overcome depression. They need to be surrounded by positive people, happy people, because happy people radiate positive vibes which makes the surrounding positive.

Medicines are fine if used for short term, but long term use of these medicines makes our body used to it and thus fades away the effects, resulting in the increase in dosage constantly. It also has its own side-effects. Stopping the medication after using it for a long period is difficult. It requires much more hard work and dedication.

How to prevent depression:

According to me, the best way to stay away from depression is to develop a hobby and follow it. For e.g. If you love to dance, make sure to take out some time every day for it, no matter how busy your schedule is. When you do something you love, it is equivalent to meditation, as during that time, it is just you and your passion. If you observe, when we do things we loved, during that span of time, our mind is free from all other thoughts. Isn't this what meditation really is?

Secondly, we should exercise on a daily basis. Fit body result in a healthy mind. Studies have shown that regular exercise decreases tension, elevates mood and has anti-anxiety effects. Exercise also helps to provide more oxygen to the brain thus helping in relieving stress and to sleep better.

So, take out some time and think, what is that one thing that really makes you happy? That you enjoy doing and makes you forget all about the world? It may be just anything. Once you have found it, do make sure to keep aside at least 15 minutes for it every day.

Instead of hiding depression, fight it, as that shows your real strength. Not everyone is able to confront depression.

Photo by Unknown

Perception Is All That Matters

Respect your perception, and also other's!!!

When we talk about perception, the first example that comes to our mind is that of a half glass of water. While some people see it as half full, others see it as half empty. Logically, both are correct, but have you ever given it a thought why is there this difference in thought?

This difference arises based on whether the person is an optimist or a pessimist. An optimist always tends to see the positive in everything, even in the worst of scenarios. I have personally met few people, who suffer from deadly diseases, but they are still happy and grateful to God for giving them the disease, as they understand that the treatment is costly but thankfully they can afford it. Had it been to someone less fortunate, it could not have been able to afford the required treatment and would have had to suffer much more.

On the other hand, a pessimist complains about everything. They feel life is too unfair to them and they are the victim of every misgiving.

The main difference between the ways an optimist or a pessimist perceives life is based on whom they compare themselves with. An optimist always considers the less fortunate than them, and hence feels blessed with whatever they have. A pessimist always compares themselves with the ones those are better off than them, and therefore are in a constant phase of self-pity and self-loathing. They don't consider, or rather fail to consider, that they themselves are better off than so many in this world.

In this world, we will find people living every type of life, but accepting our life the way it is, is the best thing we can do. If you see beggars, do you always find them crying? That is not the case, right? Even if they get one meal in a day, they are satisfied and happy. While, are rich people the most happiest in the world? The answer we all know is 'No'. Most of the rich people are the unhappy people in this world and suffer from depression, anxiety, etc. We may think they have all the money in the world and can buy whatever their heart desires, so what can make them unhappy. But, the fact is, the heart is never satisfied. No matter what you have, it always wants more. And when you have everything, the thought of losing it all eats you from within.

So, accept life the way it is. Work hard and do your best, but learn to accept the way life unfolds. We cannot change anything by cribbing about it or being sad, but if we try to be happy in every situation, facing all the shortcomings of this path called life, becomes a bit easier.

A very beautiful quote on Perception:

> *"Don't cry because it's over, smile because it happened."*
>
> Dr. Seuss

Age Is Just A Number...

You are as old as you feel within

Photo by Nick Hillier on Unsplash

My worst nightmare was about to come true. The day I dreaded the most, the day I never wanted to witness in my entire life, was just a few days away. I grew paralysed just by the thought of it. There was no way around, I just didn't have anything in my hands.

I started to lose my slept, thinking about it as the day drew closer. I looked myself in the mirror to check if I was still the same person. I frankly couldn't notice any changes; I still looked the same as I had the last year, or the year before that. Maybe had just gained few pounds, but that was very normal with me. I tend to keep gaining and losing pounds around the year. So, how could the day be approaching so soon? I still felt young within. How could the day mark that I was now old?

Finally the dreaded day arrived. At first I was scared to even open my eyes to welcome the day. But, as everyone started pouring in their wishes and love, I had to.

As soon as I opened my eyes, I was greeted with my favourite chocolate cake with big candles, which displayed "30" on it. Seeing this made my heart skip a beat, but seeing the expecting faces around me, waiting for me to cut my cake, made me feel better.

Soon I was bathed in cake and gifts as it was a milestone birthday for me, as they say. I had now entered the house of thirties. I was no longer in my twenties. I was considered to now be a grown-up; children would start calling me aunty. I would no longer be welcomed in the group of people in their twenties as I would be considered too old, and I would feel awkward in group of people elder to me. It seemed to be a very critical phase to be in.

The days following the dreaded day passed normally. I actually didn't see any change in the behaviour of people around me, as I had thought. Everything was just the same as it was before. I soon started to relax and I now no longer did mind telling people that I was 30. I looked the same, felt the same. Maybe I just had matured in my thoughts. I had 30 years of experience of life, but my body felt as young as it ever was.

I did start taking exercise and my life seriously before the age started showing, but by heart I was the same little girl, still hungry of love of her dear ones. I doubt if I will ever outgrow this.

We cannot stop ourselves from growing older every day, but what we can do instead is take our health and life seriously, enjoy ourselves as if we are still the little kid that we were when we were born and live life with no regrets. It is only then that we will realise that age is just a number. It will keep increasing every year, no matter what. It's upon us to be sad about it, or challenge it to make us feel old.

You are as old as you think you are. Age is nothing to define who you are.

Photo by Ben White on Unsplash

Keep The Child Within You Alive

Always be like a child, but not childish.

We have heard people say many times that being childlike is a quality that everyone should develop, but one must not be childish. Have you ever thought what the difference between the two is? These two may sound very similar, but what is it that makes them so different from each other?

Childlike is a quality. A child is pure at heart. It doesn't pretend. If it's hungry, it will say that. If they want something, they directly ask for it. They also say it when they don't like someone or something. They don't pretend to be what they are not. These qualities are something we all should cultivate. We don't need to pretend to be someone we are not.

The most important quality of a child is being pure by heart. We should never do something with a bad intention. If someone hurts us, it's best to say it to that person at that very moment itself. They may not have caused us pain knowingly. There are chances that the person has no clue about it. So, saying it out at the very moment helps prevent two things – firstly, saying out loud will help us take it out of our heart and lessen the pain, and secondly, it will help clear any misunderstanding. If the person knows that his deeds have caused us pain in any way, they will take care not to do it again. This simplifies life at the very instant itself.

A child won't remember what you did last summer. It forgives and forgets. It acts at the moment, and once the factor that is bothering it is removed, it forgets all about it and becomes happy again. In other words, it doesn't hold grudges. If we are able to cultivate this quality, life will become much more beautiful. We need to learn and forgive people. This is one of the child-like qualities that people take years to master. But, once we are able to master it, nothing in this world can stop us from being happy.

When we throw a child high up in the air, it laughs. This is because it trusts us by all its heart that we will catch it. This is yet another child-like quality that we should try and cultivate. Though blind-trust is not good in today's world, but trusting our near and dear ones, will ease our life to a great extent. If we don't trust anyone, it becomes very difficult to even live. So to live, we need to trust at-least few people in our lives.

A child may demand for some toy it likes. It may already have a lot of other toys, but it may still cry for the new one. This is because, as a child, it doesn't know the difference between want and need. It knows nothing about its parent's financial status. This is because it is too young to understand such practicalities of life. But, when a grown up demands for something it may not require, this behaviour is known as being childish.

A grown-up is capable of judging the difference between need and want, understanding the importance of saving for the future, still, if a grown-up doesn't seem to consider these practicalities of life, its behaviour will be considered to be childish.

An intelligent person is one who understands the difference between want and need. Need is the necessities that are required to lead a comfortable life. The basic necessities of life are - food to fill our stomach, water to quench our thirst, cloths to cover ourselves and a roof to stay safely. Beyond these, whatever we spend in is 'want'.

'Want' has no limit. It can never be satisfied. We may think that if we have a beautiful house, we will be happy. But once we have the house, we may begin to feel the need of some furniture. Till we don't buy that furniture, our mind won't be at rest. Once we have purchased the furniture that we so felt was really required, we may start wanting a car. So 'want' doesn't have any end. It just goes on and on. If we believe we are going to be happy once our wish is fulfilled, this is where we are wrong. We may feel happy for some time once our wish is fulfilled, but the next moment, our heart will be yearning for something else. Those who give in to this 'want' are childish. In such scenario, what is the difference between a child and a grown-up? What is considered to be innocence in a child is ignorance in a grown-up. Childish is a quality that is expected and accepted in a child, but not in a grown-up.

The beauty of being childlike is very well explained in the below quote:

> *To be more childlike, you don't have to give up being an adult. The fully integrated person is capable of being both an adult and a child simultaneously. Recapture the childlike feelings of wide-eyed excitement, spontaneous appreciation, cutting loose, and being full of awe and wonder at this magnificent universe. - Wayne Dyer*

So be proud if someone calls you childlike, but if someone calls you childish, remember childish is equivalent to being immature, and that's not a quality you would like to have. So being childlike and mature is the best combination.

Photo by Omar Lopez on Unsplash

Every 'BODY' Is Beautiful

There is no such thing as a perfect body.

The world is full of people of varying shapes, sizes and colours, but defining a specific shape, size and colour to be the symbol of 'perfect body' is impossible.

Every person has a unique body structure, based on which the best weight and shape for the person will change. Everyone is unique. The only thing that should matter while deciding if we are fit is that we don't feel tired and drained out all the time. A person will get tired quickly only if it is either overweight, or underweight.

A 6 feet tall person may weight 50kg or 70kg. If the person is able to carry on with its normal day-to-day activities without any difficulty, then it is fit. We may look slim even at 70kgs or have flab even if we are only 50kgs. It all depends on our height and body structure. Some people have heavy bones, so even though they may weigh more than others, it is fine for them. Just by calling them fat, based on weight, is not correct.

We should aim at being fit and not skinny, and that is indicated if we have good stamina, irrespective of our weight.

In normal cases, people try and keep themselves fit. When we see someone who is underweight or overweight, we should understand that it's not by choice. It's how their body functions. Some people eat a lot, but still don't put on weight. This is because it's in their genes. Whereas, other may eat very less, but still gain weight. In such cases it's the body's mechanism of converting food to energy that is slow.

Many weight issues are also due to certain diseases like Hypo/Hyper Thyroid, Diabetes, etc., but this doesn't give us the right to judge people. We don't know what the other may be going through. We should just be proud of ourselves, no matter how we look. We should not be shy of ourselves, be it for our body or our looks. We need to start loving ourselves before we can expect others to love us.

A woman, who has stretch-marks all over her stomach, shows that she has the ability to give birth to a new life. She has nothing to be ashamed of or to hide. She needs to be proud of those stretch marks as she has the capability, which many don't. Many just try for years to attain motherhood, but without success. She should be thankful to God for it. So aren't these stretch-marks beautiful.

An obese woman may work hard and loose those excess pounds, but this result in loose skin all over her body. Does she need to feel shy about it? No, she doesn't. It shows how hard she has worked, her dedication to lose those pounds, to become fit. Not everyone has that kind of dedication and determination. So aren't these loose skins beautiful.

We shouldn't be ashamed of our body no matter however it is. Nobody has the right to judge it. If we are not satisfied with our body, we need to work towards it, but for the betterment of our-self, and not harm our-self in anyway by comparing it with others. If we try and change it only based on comparison, we may end up harming our health, than doing any good for it. We may not realise it at the moment and even be happy about it, but it will lead to several health issues as we grow old. That time we will have nothing in our hands to change.

If suppose we have a pear-shaped figure, but we want an hour-glass figure, we need to understand that it's not possible, as our body structure is different. No matter how hard we try, we cannot change it. But both are beautiful in their own ways. So instead, being happy with our-self is the best we can do. If we love our-self, accept our-self the way we are, others will be forced to love us, and then, actually it won't even bother us if they don't.

A person with self-confidence, pure heart and a smiling face is the most beautiful person on earth, and that is what attracts others to them. Our body is just a home to our soul for as long as we are alive. So it's just the soul that should be beautiful. When we die, this body will be converted to ashes anyway. So does it even make sense to worry about how this body looks?

So wear whatever you want to and be confident about yourself. If you are fine with it, you feel confident in it, and then who are others to bother. It's your body and so it's you who should decide what you want to wear. As long as you feel comfortable in it, it is the best for you and you look beautiful.

This is rightly stated here:

> *Acceptance is being able to feel beautiful in whatever you feel comfortable in.*
>
> \- Barbie Ferreira

Photo by Andy Tootell on Unsplash

Just Say No!

You are not helping yourself by saying yes all the time

Once I went for a two-day trip with my friends. We were 8 of us, so we rented a van for ourselves for the entire duration, so that we could cover more places easily. We all were very excited for the day. We packed all our stuffs that we thought we might require. The path to the destination was said to be mesmerising, so each of us packed our cameras to capture loads of photos of the entire trip.

Soon the most awaited day arrived. We were to leave early in the morning and gathered around our vehicle right at 5 in the morning. None of us were able to sleep that night due to excitement. I could even feel butterflies in my stomach.

The driver informed us that there was a forecast of rain that day, so it would be better to adjust our luggage inside instead of tying it on the roof of the van. We had no other option but to agree. We were supposed to sit in the following order – 1 beside the driver's seat, 3 on the seat behind the driver's row and the remaining 4 at the back (2 on each side facing each other). So some of our luggage was dumped on the floor of the front seats, but majority was dumped on the floor of the backseat (as it was more spacious).

So, as decided, till we arrived at our first stop, which was 4 hours from our current location, I agreed to sit at the backseat along with 3 others. We were supposed to have our breakfast there and then continue with our journey forward. There, those who wanted to exchange their seats could do so.

Finally we hit the road. After driving for 1 hour or so, we got to see picturesque view of the road ahead, with mountains on one side, and the river on the other. It was seriously breath-taking. I tried taking few pictures, but as the window was behind me, I had to turn around to capture some. The space, already being restricted by that entire luggage, was making it very difficult and gave me a backache. So, I decided to collect the pictures captured by my friends instead and convinced myself that I would capture some amazing pictures later when I got to sit in the front.

Soon, we arrived at the first stop and finally we were able to stretch our legs. There we had some amazing fulfilling breakfast and were again ready to proceed with our trip. This time the 4 of us, who were sitting at the back, got the front seats and the others moved to our seats. I was happy, as finally I could capture some good shots to share with my family. Suddenly, just after half an hour of travelling further, one of my friends, now sitting at the backseat, asked the driver to stop. She complained that she has motion sickness and so would have to sit in the front by the window. Since other were not ready to sacrifice their seats, I agreed to give her mine and move back again, with the condition that the rest of us would keep shuffling our places at different intervals.

After travelling for 2 hours, I asked if someone was willing to exchange their place with me, but none agreed. They pleaded me to sit till we stopped for lunch and then they would reshuffle. I couldn't say no to my friends, so I agreed. I kept my camera inside.

After another 3 long hours, we took another break for a late lunch. Now we were just 2 hours away from our destination. So, not wanting to waste much time, we quickly had our lunch and proceeded to our van. By the time I reached the van, others had already taken up the best seats leaving the back one for me. I tried to persuade one of them to exchange seats, but they said it's just 2 hours more, and so to adjust once more. Again, disheartened, I agreed.

Soon we reached our destination, but all my excitement had vanished by then. During the rest of our trip, I just remained silent and let others have their way. I was way too hurt by the whole incident. On our way back, I voluntarily sat at the backseat for the entire duration, and no one seemed to care.

What do you think, whose fault was it? They were mean and selfish, you would all agree. But, read the story once more. Wasn't I as much at fault as them? Didn't I let them take me for granted? Had I been able to hold my stand and not be pleaded by them every time, then I would have had an amazing time with loads of good memories captured as well. It was just because I couldn't say '**No**'.

If a person really cares for you, they will respect it when you say 'No' for something. If they don't, then we don't need to care about what they will think anyways.

We can't change what someone thinks about us, what we can instead do is, respect ourselves and give more importance to ourselves, than we give to others. We need to say 'No' when we don't wish to do a thing.

This is very well stated in the below quote:

> *Love yourself enough to set boundaries. Your time and energy are precious. You get to choose how you use it. You teach people how to treat you by deciding what you will and won't accept.*
>
> Anna Taylor

So, say 'No' when required. You don't need to feel guilty for saying 'No'.

Photo by Shane Rounce on Unsplash

The Great Fall

I was heading towards my end

I am finally here. Since I was a kid, Paris had been my dream destination to visit with my lover. During my teenage years, I had watched many romantic movies and read various novels, all about love and Paris. It was all sketched in my mind like a movie. He, surprising me by taking me to Paris, then he kissing me for the first time under the Eiffel Tower to him finally propose to me at the most romantic spot on the planet. It was just picture perfect.

My dream was about to be changed into reality, the only difference being the lover here is my husband (so first kiss ticked off), but it doesn't lessen the excitement of being here even a tiny bit. I was in all moods to replay the movie that had been on my mind for so long.

We had planned of staying at the city for 4 days, so we decided to visit Eiffel tower on day 2. The first day we just wanted to stroll around and visit the famous museum – The Louvre Museum. None of us normally visited museums, but this one specially held my interest, as I am a great fan of Leonardo Da Vinci and specifically, his famous painting of Mona Lisa. I wanted to see the mysterious smile, which is the main attraction of this painting, with my own eye.

Having landed there at 10 a.m. itself, and the hotel room only being available after 2 p.m., we decide to drop our luggage on the hotel and left to visit the museum. Soon we reach the museum and were able to skip the long line, thanks to the Paris Museum Pass. It was huge and beautiful. I was pleasantly surprised that the museum was the home to a large number of beautiful original works of great artists, apart from Mona Lisa. It was breath-taking. We didn't realise how quickly the time flew by and it was only at 3 in the afternoon that we realised, as we had started to feel hungry. So, we quickly hogged our lunch that we had got along and proceeded back to our hotel to freshen up.

We took a lazy stroll around the city in the evening, had our dinner by the roadside restaurants and retired to our room little early as we were tired with the travelling and jet-lag. We had planned of visiting Sainte Chapelle in the morning, the next day. From there we were to proceed towards Eiffel Tower, roaming around and having our lunch in the garden in front of the Eiffel Tower and had booked our tickets to go to the top of it at around 7 in the evening. I even wanted to get a picture clicked of us kissing with just the Eiffel Tower behind us, like the ones we see in movies.

Next day I woke up, after being shaken rigorously by my husband, shouting that we had overslept. I hurriedly checked my watch only to find that it was already 4 in the afternoon. We didn't have time to visit Sainte Chapelle and would have to directly proceed to Eiffel Tower, if we were to make it to the top on time, considering the queue.

I quickly showered and got ready, grabbed something to eat and soon we were on our way to Eiffel Tower. There was a massive queue, so we decided on visiting the garden, after our trip to the top of it. Soon it was our turn and we got into the lift. At the second level, we got into another lift and soon the lift halted as we reached its peak. I could hear my heartbeat loud and clear. This was the moment I had been waiting for my entire life. My husband got off the lift before me and offered me his hand. I could feel my cheeks turning red as I lifted my hand to take his. But suddenly, he disappeared, and all the people around. Slowly, I could see the lift disappearing along with the Eiffel Tower. There was nothing below me and I began to fall down, and down, and down. I was sure I wasn't going to survive this great fall, and just prayed for it to be less painful. I couldn't hear my screams but could feel the gravity pulling me down in great force. It was, as I was about to hit the ground, that I got up with a start, just to realise that it had all been a dream. I drew a long breath of relief and was all sweaty. My excitement to visit the Eiffel Tower had made me dream about it, to this extent.

I checked the time. It was just 5 in the morning. We had plenty of time to start the day. I chuckled within, thinking that this time we wouldn't be late and visit all that we had planned for the day. The rest of our trip was spent as planned and Paris made me fall for it more than I could ever have had imagined. It was just mesmerising.

When we got back, I was fully satisfied as our visit to Paris, specifically the Eiffel Tower, had been perfect with the perfect shot captured, like the one I wanted, by a very talented couple we meet at the garden. I had it framed and hung it in our bedroom. But, whenever I recall my dream of '**the great fall**', it still gives me the shivers.

Photo by Angels Vicente on Unsplash

How To Survive Old Age?

Can old people live a happy life?

In one of my blogs, I had mentioned that, in order to live a peaceful and happy retirement life, we should have three things in life, i.e. Health, Wealth and Friends. Someone asked me, what if any or all of these is missing in a person's life? Does that mean they have nothing left to stay happy or live for?

I got into thinking as each of these seems to be of great importance in itself. We cannot even think of living through our old age if any of these is missing, as when we are old and retired, how do we earn money and take care of ourselves? At this stage of life, people become physically weak. We cannot be as productive as we used to be when we were younger. These seem to be the basic necessities of life. What do you think? Does it mean end of life?

Then I thought about my grandma. She is sick and old, yet she seems happy. How is that possible? It was then that I realised that I had been missing the obvious, it's family. She has her family with her, to take care of her and to accompany her. All her basic needs are taken care of by her family. She had given up her entire life for her family without expecting anything in return; now, it is their turn to do the same for her, when she is no longer physically able to take care of herself. She doesn't need to worry about money or friends for company. Having her family in this phase of her life is all she could ever have hoped for.

Love is a two-sided affair. If you really love someone, the person will, in-turn, love you. The greater the love you shower on them, they tend to give you the same. We don't need to be vocal about our love. It is displayed in the way we care for the other, without expecting anything in return. If we do expect something in return, then it is not actual love, as then it is not pure. This is what happens in a family. The children grow up to reflect the love they had received while growing up.

We see many cases now-a-days, where the children disown their old parents. This is not right, but what is it that made them do it in the first place. Moreover, this is not the case in every family. So, what was the difference that made few children to disown their parents when they most needed them? It's love.

As very well stated in the below quote:

> *Those who love deeply never grow old; they may die of old age, but they die young.*
>
> –Dorothy Canfield Fisher

Love doesn't grow old with age. How we treat our children, how we make them feel in their growing years, is how they treat us when we are old and weak. The way a child is treated, leaves a life-long impression on them. If a child is constantly told that they are dumb, at some point in time, they tend to believe it. They are deprived of love of their parents. So, when their parents grow old, they don't feel any bond or connection with them. They began to see them as an unnecessary burden, of which they try to get rid of. As they were never emotionally attached, the child doesn't feel guilty of disowning their parents, because they never felt that their parents had ever accepted them.

So, to live a happy life, we need to love unconditionally, be it family, friends, colleagues or any person we come across in this path of life. We should spread love wherever possible, because the more love we give, the more we get. If we give our unconditional love to someone, the person will in-turn love us, without our even expecting it. It's like a magnet. It pulls people towards us. They cannot hate us, no matter how much they try.

This is what this entire universe is based on. What you give is what you get. Give love and you will get love in return, give hate and hate will surround you.

So, it's completely on our hands how we want our old age to be. Though some misfortunes are inevitable, what we can do is, love unconditionally, exercise daily to try and stay fit and always remember to keep some money aside for our future. This way, when we grow old, we cannot be sure that we will have good health and wealth, but what we can be sure of is that we will always be surrounded with people whom we love, and who love us in return. Then, old age won't seem so difficult to live, other than it being just another phase of life.

Photo by Hans Vivek on Unsplash

The Uninvited Guest

When I was very young, every summer break, we would head to our maternal grandma's house. I used to love going there, as, being the youngest, I was pampered a lot. And moreover, who doesn't like a holiday full of delicious home-made delicacies to eat???

I prefer salted over sweet, and as my grandma knew this, she would fill her glass jars with various types of chips and roasted split peas (being my favourite), before I would reach. Every day, little after breakfast, I would sit in the stairs of her balcony, with a bowl of roasted split peas, and have it at a leisurely pace. I would toss each one of them up in the air, and try to catch it with my mouth, spilling some in the process.

One such day, as I was passing by the balcony, a little after eating the split peas, I observed that the ones I had spilled were not there. I was convinced that grandma must have cleared them, and soon forgot all about it as the day progressed.

For the next few days, the pattern continued, and it made me suspicious, as I would never see my grandma cross the balcony. Even if she had, she would have at least told me once to eat properly and not waste food this way. This didn't seem right somehow and I decided to investigate it myself.

So the next day, I purposely spilled few more split peas and hid behind the wall to see who was this uninvited guest having my peas. I didn't have to wait long. Just few minutes later, I saw many tiny ants march towards the spilled peas in a line. As the size of the pea was too big as compared to them, they formed a group of 3–4 ants to carry each pieces in coordination. They carried these to small holes on the side of the stairs. Soon every piece was carried into the holes and the place was left clean.

That night I told my grandma what I saw. She smiled, and explained me- *"Ants are the hardest working insects. A single ant can carry weight much more that itself. They carry the food to their homes to eat and store away the excess, to help them survive when they don't get any. We can learn a lot from an ant".*

I was very impressed by this. It made me want to help them. So, the next day, while I was eating the split peas, I purposefully stuffed few in those holes for the ants, as I was worried who would feed them when I went back home.

Few days later I left for home, satisfied with myself and with a number of life lessons the ants had taught me.

So, what can we learn from these ants?

- Firstly, we see the importance of team work. As the split pea was impossible for a single ant to carry, they overcame this difficulty by forming groups and thus making it possible for them to carry it, and at a lesser time. We find it difficult to work in teams as we are always trying to prove our-self better than the other. We don't hesitate to betray the other, if we feel we will have some benefit out of it. We are selfish.
- We can learn discipline from them. Ants always walk in a single line. They don't try to overtake the other to reach the food quicker. If we humans follow the same, our life will be much more meaningful and simpler. We always try to get ahead of the one before us, sometime using the wrong way. We are always at competition with the other. While competition to a limit is healthy

and good for self-betterment, too much of it can destroy us.

- They are good at managing resources. They eat what is required, and store the rest for later. Thus, in event of some calamity, they won't die of hunger. They safe for future. On the other hand, we human beings, spend on useless things while we have the money, due to which, we are not left with any when we really need it. We give in to the **want** rather than the actual **need**.

This is rightly stated in the below words:

> *I think everybody should study ants. They have an amazing four-part philosophy. Never give up, look ahead, stay positive and do all you can.*
>
> Jim Rohn

These, if followed by us human beings, will help us lead a better life. To live in peace and harmony, only use/buy what is necessary and save the rest for the future. Sounds to be so simple, but difficult to follow, isn't it?

Photo by Elena Saharova on Unsplash

Is Retirement The Worst Phase Of Life?

Does retirement mean the end of life?

One day, as I returned from office, I saw my grandfather sitting on his usual spot, i.e. in front of the television, but something seemed unusual. He didn't seem to be watching the television, but, instead, was lost in some deep thought. His forehead had few deep wrinkles that seemed more defined now, as he sat engrossed in his thoughts. His mouth had some grim expression, and he looked oh so sad. Seeing him like this broke my heart into pieces.

I approached him and sat beside him. I took his hands on mine. It was then, as if he came back to reality with a sudden jerk. He seemed both surprised and pleased to see me. It was clear he hadn't notice me coming in. He asked me, a little embarrassed, that how long I had been there. I just rubbed his hands in reassurance and lied that I had just entered. He seemed visibly relieved.

We started talking about general stuff while he inquired me about my day and what exciting things did I do during the day. I gave him a detailed overview about my day and faked some challenges that I faced in office and how I resolved them. He seemed pleased.

As he began to come back to his usual self, I took the opportunity and asked him the question that had been lingering on my mind since the moment I entered-"*What were you thinking about grandpa? You looked very sad, is something disturbing you?*" He considered my question for some time, while his smile vanished. His face turned sad once again. I doubted if he was going to answer my question, but I also knew he loved me and could never say no to me, so I made a puppy face and urged him a little more. Finally his body relaxed a little and he gave out a long sigh. I knew I had my way.

So, this is what he said:

> *"I know I must be a burden for you all. All I do is sit around the whole day. I have nothing to do, nowhere to go and nobody to talk to. My life is finished. I have never felt so useless. I hate being retired".*

Isn't this generally the thought when you hear about being retired? Old, sick with nothing left to do. We hardly even prefer spending time with them. We prefer partying over sitting and talking to them.

What we forget is being retired doesn't really require us to be useless. It actually marks the end of a phase where we have done our duty and life is now giving us the time to enjoy it to the fullest. Now we don't need to worry about some nasty boss we have to please, appraisals and all the worldly possessions. We are the boss of our lives.

This is the time to fulfil all that we have dreamt for and spend all those hard earned money. Go on trips, eat all that we love and thank the almighty for this day as everyone is not lucky enough to get the opportunity to live a life of retirement.

We should in-fact plan our retirement. You must be wondering what this is even supposed to mean. What

I want to say here is that, we should save well for our retirement, make few real friends and exercise every day in order to keep ourselves fit, because this is all that we will require once we are retired. We need **money** to travel and to fund our daily needs, **health** to not be dependent on anyone, and **friends** for company.

On top of all these is will-power - The will-power to live; the will-power to make each day better than the previous; the will-power to never give up no matter how hard life may seem.

We should retire with satisfaction knowing that we have achieved what we deserved. We have worked hard all these years and done our best and now is the time to celebrate.

We always hear people say that building a hobby in life is very important. Have you ever thought about what is its significance? The simple reason is that, having a hobby helps us to look forward to something when we retire. While we are working, it's difficult to take out enough time to work on our hobby, but once we are retired, we have all the time in the world and engaging our-self in it will make us forget about time itself. Days won't seem hard to pass as when we do something we love, time flies.

"Retire from work, but not from life."

M.K. Soni

So, retirement doesn't symbolise the end of life, in-fact it's the beginning to a life we always wanted to live.

Photo by Natalya Zaritskaya on Unsplash

Is Nuclear Family Better Than Joint Family?

From a couple's perspective

I have had the opportunity to live in both Nuclear and Joint family, and if this question is put up before me, I would really don't know what to choose.

In most cases, for a girl to be specific, she either moves to a nuclear family after marriage, or if she has been living in a joint family, she may consider moving in to a joint family, even after marriage. For me, the case was the complete opposite. I used to stay in a nuclear family, and after marriage, I moved in to a joint family.

So, choosing one over the other would truly be wrong, as both the type of family has some pros and cons. It's like choosing between sugar and salt. Each has its own unique flavour which cannot be compared or substituted.

Now, when I look back, I can surely say what each is like.

During my growing up years, I have always watched my parents very open with each other, and us. We would discuss everything and anything possible in the world, in the presence of each other. We would be least bothered about what we wear when we were at home, or how we sat and our house could be as messy as it may be. Our parents would hold hands in our presence and not shy away to display their love for each other. Whenever we would expect any guest, it was then that we got into a parade to make the house and ourselves presentable.

While, after I got married, staying in a joint family brought forward its own limitations. I had to be presentable every-time and would have to sit properly, with my legs down in front of my in-laws, in order to show them respect. It was considered indecent if I displayed love towards my husband in the presence of the elders, in any form, be it as simple a gesture as holding hands. I couldn't throw things around the house and had to limit my things to my room. I was even expected to keep my room presentable every-time. Everything I did, I had to keep the family in mind, and act accordingly.

By now, you must be thinking why is it difficult for me to choose, as it clearly shows nuclear family to be more liveable. But that is not the case. Till now we have only talked about the pros of a nuclear family. But, it has a long list of cons as well, just like a joint family.

In a nuclear family, it's just the two of us, i.e. the husband and the wife. The children come in, at a later stage. With only two people in a house, we tend to feel very lonely, as we don't have anyone else to talk to, and how much can we talk among ourselves. As the management of the house is entirely on us, when we get tired, even a small act can fire us up and we end up exploding at the other. What you cook is what you eat. You cannot expect, that on days when you return late and tired from office, to get prepared food. We need to cook our own food or eat out (which is not a very feasible solution for an everyday routine). In the absence of the other, we are left all alone.

In these cases, having a joint family is the best thing that can happen to us. We are never alone; there will always be someone or the other. We have people to care for us. As the number of helping hands increase, managing the house seems less tiresome and can even be enjoyable at times. When we get late at work, we may expect food cooked and kept for us. On a funny note, having a dine-out becomes more enjoyable as you have several dishes to try from.

In a nuclear family, when the wife is expecting, it becomes very difficult for the husband to handle everything on his own. It takes a toll on him. And once she delivers the baby, she needs to stay at home and take care of the baby all by herself, while the husband earns to fund for the increase in expense.

On the other hand, in a joint family, there are others to help the husband at this stage of life. Once the baby is delivered, there are more people to take care of it, thus giving some rest to the mother. She and the child are well cared after. As the child grows, she has the option to start working again, knowing that she has a family to take care of her child in her absence. The entire process of motherhood becomes less tiring and more fun.

So, let life decide which type of family is best for us. We should just accept it and live to the fullest. Life is best the way it is.

Photo by Robbie Noble on Unsplash

Why I Left My Dream Company

I was in love with the company the very first day I step foot on it

It was the last year of my college. It was that time of the year when campus recruitment process was supposed to commence. We all were excited and nervous as it would be our first experience at giving interviews, in order to get into a good company. We were about to enter the second phase of our life – Work Life, where we were just getting over with the first phase i.e. Student Life. We were going to become professionals. We were beginning to understand how important it was.

One fine Wednesday morning, as I entered college, I heard a lot of commotion going on. On enquiring with my friends, I got to know that the first company had been scheduled to visit our college for the placement process. It was to come on Friday. Having just 2 days to prepare, I first started with reading about the company as, till then, I hadn't heard of its name. I soon came to know that it was, supposedly, the third best company in the world. If I got through it, my whole life would be set. The first round would be an aptitude test, so I started preparing for it.

Soon it was Friday, and students in thousands entered the hall where the aptitude test was supposed to be held. Seeing the huge number I really got nervous, as it made my chance of getting through even less. I decided not to back out and at-least give it a try. I had nothing to lose, and it would further help me be better prepared for other companies' aptitude test. It would help me understand the pattern.

The representatives of the company soon arrived and distributed us the question papers, with all the instructions we were required to follow. The questions were well thought of, and I had to rack my brain and apply all my analytical skills to solve it, to the best of my capabilities. Soon it was time and we submitted our answer sheets. They informed us that they would validate it and inform our college's Placement Department about the result.

After the test, on enquiring with my other batch-mates, I got a little disheartened, as everyone seemed to have performed like or better than me. I just left the result on God, believing he will do what is best for me.

On Monday, we attended college as usual. The day was proceeding as expected when one of my friends, came to me and said she had some news for me. I was clueless about what it could be and asked her. It was then she informed me that only 7 students had cleared the aptitude test and I was one of them. I couldn't believe my ears and jumped with delight.

The days after this, passed swiftly with me clearing both the round of interviews that followed and was the only one to be selected from my entire college. My happiness knew no bounds. My parents were so proud of me.

College got over and it was my first day at work. The moment I entered the company's campus, I fell in love with it. It was huge with large gardens all around. I even started dreaming of getting old working at the company.

The initial 2 years just flew by like a dream. I say like a dream, because, everything was so perfect and I just couldn't have expected more. I loved working there and the people were good. Moreover, they even provided delicious free meals.

After two years, I was incorporated as a permanent employee and my salary was raised in many folds. It was then that the actual problems began. First, the project we were working on was allocated to another team, while my team was assigned a new project, which used a new technology about which I didn't have any idea. My team members were reshuffled and I found myself with all new team members and a new manager.

At first, we were given an overview of the new project. It was difficult for me to grasp as the technology was very new for me, while the other team members had already worked on that technology before, so it wasn't a problem for them. Soon after, the customer issues started pouring in and each of us were expected to close them at the earliest.

Finally, I decided to approach my manager and ask him to provide me with the training to understand the new technology, because with so many customer issues pouring in, nobody had the time to guide me. But the manager refused, and instead handed me a large module to learn and work on, all by myself, that too within a very limited time. I didn't have any other option, so I started working on it based on what little I understood, but to no avail.

Gradually, the behaviour of my team-members grew toxic as they began to taunt me that I couldn't contribute on fixing the customer issues and they were overloaded due to it. They looked down on me and made me feel I wasn't qualified enough to be there. I was getting depressed by the day. I started to dread going to office every morning.

So, I decided to talk to the HR, to ask if she could help me, because the behaviour of the manager and the team mates were not justifiable. It was also the company's policy to provide its employee with any training they ask for, yet I was being deprived of it.

The HR seemed to understand my concerns, and promised that she would get back to me. But, on the contrary, she, being close to my manager, told him everything and they together plotted to throw me out of the company before I could say it to anyone else. They called me to a meeting and offered me an only solution out, if I wanted to stay in the company.

I had already had had enough and I declined their offer. I believe mental peace is greater than anything else. The environment there had become too toxic to stick around and I submitted my resignation.

That day I learned something. No matter how good a company is, if the people or work is not good, it is not good for you.

As rightly expressed:

> *A highly paid, highly motivated employee who is not allowed to work with his full potential is like a Ferrari which is not allowed out of the garage.*
>
> – Charbel Tadros

Silence: A Secret Weapon

How is silence a weapon?

Photo by Kristina Flour on Unsplash

When I was small, my father used to recite to me a lot of stories. He has a stock full of stories. He has like a new story to explain every aspects of life, thus making it more interesting and easier to understand. I would love listening to his stories as a child, and I still do.

One such day, he told me this amazing story, which I still remember word by word. The story goes as follows:

There was a small village where people used to live in huts, very close to each other. On one of these huts lived a husband and a wife. They were in their forties and had been married for years. In those villages, girls and boys were married off at a very young age. It was believed that since they grew up together, they would have better understanding among themselves and get used to each other at a very young age.

This couple, however, didn't get along at all. It began with them fighting some days, to them fighting every day. They would shout at each other on top of their voices, call each other names and sometimes even throw utensils at each other.

As the huts were situated close to each other, the neighbours would have a hard time with the entire racket they created. Moreover, they didn't want their children to hear and learn the curses. They tried talking to the couple many time, but to no avail.

Once, a Saint visited the village. The village ladies convinced the women to meet the Saint, as he would surely have some solution to help her regain peace with her husband. The women agreed and visited the Saint that very day.

The Saint patiently heard the woes of the women, and once she finished, he asked her to do just one thing – " Fill your mouth with water every-time your husband is around. Take care not to swallow it or spit it. Do this every day and have patience. All will be well".

The woman was excited to test what the Saint had just asked her to do. So, the first day she filled her mouth with water as soon as her husband entered. He, as usual, started shouting and cursing her. She too wanted to revolt, but with her mouth filled with water, she couldn't utter a word. The husband grew angrier when she didn't react, but it still didn't make the wife fight back.

This happened for a few days, and slowly, the husband started to curse less, till he got tired of cursing alone and finally stopped it altogether.

What do you think was the reason that the husband stopped cursing his wife? Why would they go on and on in the beginning? The simple reason is, in the beginning, as his wife responded to his shouting, he would instead shout and curse even more. He knew it affected her and that's what he wanted. Both wanted to win the argument. Isn't this what we all want when we are angry?

In the latter case, when the wife couldn't respond, as she had her mouth filled with water, at first the husband got irritated as to why were his words not affecting her? He was getting affected by her silence. As the days passed, he noticed that his words were falling on deaf ears and it didn't affect the wife. No matter how hard he tried, the wife didn't say a word. Finally he got tired of shouting alone, and so he stopped.

So, now we see what the Saint's motive was. He used the wife's silence as a secret weapon to stop the husband from cursing and bring back normalcy in their lives. This is the strength of silence.

Silence speaks more than words. It also has a greater impact than words. When a mother beats or scolds her child, it may not commit the same mistake once, but it may commit the same mistake the next time. Whereas, if the mother punishes her child by not talking to it for some time, that is the worst punishment for it. A child can bear the beatings and scolding of their parent, but they cannot bear to know that their parents are not talking to them. Their silence causes the child more pain and fear, than their actions. Silence is considered to be the best punishment for a child. This fear prevents the child from committing the same mistake again.

When we hurt someone knowingly or unknowingly, and the person doesn't say a thing, it makes us feel much guiltier than what we would have felt if the person had taken it out on us.

Silence of a person we love, is very hard to handle. Words help us understand what is going on within the person, their feelings or anything that is disturbing them. Whereas, if a person is silent, we don't know what is going on within them and this affect us more. It makes us feel as if we are losing our hold on that person.

This is well-stated in the below quote:

> *It's a difficult competition against silence, because silence is a perfect language, the only language which says with no words.*
>
> Eduardo Galeano

So, don't consider a person, who is silent, to be weak. Silence is, at most time, a symbol of immense strength within. A person, who is silent during hardships, is the one who can overcome any battle of life.

But an alteration to this, however, is if a person is silent, even after witnessing something wrong being done to others, is the most awful person in the world.

So, practice and master using this weapon of silence, to improve your life and that of others, but not to harm anyone in any way.

Photo by Lesly Juarez on Unsplash

How To Be Happy

Is it difficult to be happy?

"...No, I told you multiple times that I am fine. Now please leave me alone" – I said to my husband.

Yesterday was our 5th Anniversary. I believed it to be a very special day as we had completed half a decade together, with many more to come. It was the first of the many milestones. Like every other married couples, we have had our share of love, happiness, misunderstandings, fights, but only to make our bond stronger. I had really been looking forward to this day.

I am the kind of person who loves reading romantic novels, cry after watching an emotional movie and love fairy-tales. I knew my husband was just the opposite of me (through experience of-course), but one cannot stop from dreaming, right?? I had this expectation that since, it was the first milestone of our lives; he would have planned something special for me, like a candle-light dinner or something. I had even purchased a sexy backless dress for the occasion.

Finally the day arrived. It started just like I would have expected it to, with a big bouquet of bright red roses lying on my bed side table, just as I opened my eyes. I turned towards where my husband was lying, and found him wide awake and staring at me. He kissed me and we wished each other. I thanked him for the beautiful roses.

Then we got ready for work. When I went down, there was a chocolate cake waiting to greet us and our family members were standing there with open arms. We rushed forward to meet them and take their blessings, cut the cake and accepted the gifts they had got us. Finally we left for office.

On the way, none of us talked about what we would be doing in the evening, and I took it as a cue that he had certainly planned something. With great difficulty I survived through the day at office, as the butterflies in my stomach were killing me. I hated suspense. It was just too much for me to handle. Whenever I read any suspense novel, I would, most of the times, read the end, just to know that my favourite character isn't dead.

Soon office hours came to an end and I headed home. My husband usually comes a little late, so I took the time to relax. I was expecting that he would call and ask me to be ready, but he didn't. So I got ready, just in-case he wanted to surprise me and gives me no time to change. I wanted to look my best.

Slowly time passed and soon it was 10 p.m. I was getting impatient and finally called him to ask when he would be coming back home. But what he replied, just broke my hopes into pieces. *"I will get very late at work today so please don't wait for me. I will call for something for dinner. You have yours"*- he said. I could hardly speak as emotions took over me, and I just disconnected the call. I changed and directly went to bed, without having dinner.

Next day I was too disgusted with him even to talk and gave him the cold treatment. He kept asking me what's wrong, but I just didn't want to talk about it.

What do you think was the main reason for my sadness? Was it that he didn't take me for dinner or that he didn't even come early to spend few precious moments with me on our special day? No, it's none of these. The main reason was expectations. We all have high expectations from others, from ourselves and expectations always hurt.

In the morning I was happy, because I hadn't expected the bouquet and the yummy cake. It was unexpected and so it made me feel like I was on top of the world. But for the evening, I had expected a lot from him, knowing that his work nature was uncertain and it required long hours. I was in my own dream world and not wanting to believe the realities of life.

So, what is the most important thing required to be happy? **It is not having any expectations from anyone.** We need to take life as it comes, and live for today. Do something for someone, and you will observe how this makes you happy. The little things of life makes a person really happy and we need to start admiring them.

Another important thing is pouring our heart out. If something is bothering us and someone approaches us that time and asks if we are fine, say *"No, I am not fine"*. Sharing our feelings with someone helps us to feel lighter. The person may not be able to provide any solution for it, but just getting it out of our heart, makes us feel better.

If we are feeling sad, we should cry it out. Some believe that crying will show that they are weak, but that's not true. Instead, being able to cry our heart out, actually displays our strength. We will always feel better once we cry it out and be able to reason things better.

So, live for the moment, be satisfied with yourself and be happy always.

> *"A great obstacle to happiness is to expect too much happiness."*
>
> – By Bernard de Fontenelle

Photo by Becca Tapert on Unsplash

Who Are Friends?

Not everybody we meet end up being our friend

Graduation was the best phase of my life. This was where I met my soul mates, i.e. my friends. During those days, I would consider all my batch-mates to be my friend. Now when I look back, I realise, apart from a few, the rest were just my batch-mates, not friends.

When we start working at some company, the people we work with are known as colleagues. Why is it so? It is because we are professionally linked to them but not personally or emotionally. Our relation exists only while we are at office, or wherever office work is evolved. They don't mean any more than that. Once we change our company, we get a new set of colleagues and most of the old ones are forgotten.

But, there are these few special ones who always stay in our lives. Be it from school, college or workplace, they always stay connected. It doesn't matter if we are together or miles apart, it's the heart that is connected, such that whenever we meet them, every day or once in a while, we always are able to start from where we last left. The time gap in between doesn't matter. Such people are known as 'Friends'.

> *"True friendship comes when the silence between two people is comfortable."*
>
> David Tyson

We hear people term friends as 'the real friend' and 'the false friend'. I personally don't believe in any such thing as a 'false friend'. If we call someone our friend, it's only the real ones, else why do we have terms like classmates, batch-mates or colleagues. The false friends, as people refer them, are just people whose path crosses our path of life for a brief interval of time. They are there just to play their part in our life, but we shouldn't allow them to affect our life in any way. We should just learn the lesson life wants to teach us and move on.

On the other hand, 'Friends' are:

- People who help bring out the best in us.
- We may experience a sense of deja vu when we are with them.
- They seem to understand the true us, and we can just be our own selves in their presence. They don't try to change us
- They don't judge us ever.
- They will always support us, but not when we are wrong
- They are our go-to person for the most precious set of advises
- It doesn't matter if we don't talk to them every day, we know in our hearts that they will be there when we truly need them
- They are the same in front of you as they are behind you
- In short, they are our siblings from another mother

Finding such friends isn't easy. But if we have them, we have the real treasure of the world. We always have the satisfaction that there is someone who knows the real us and loves us for the person we are, that we will never be alone.

You must have heard the saying:

> *A woman may stay without a husband, but not without her girlfriends*

I completely vouch for it. Men and Women are very different in the way they think. When a woman shares her feelings with a man, he may not understand the gravity of it. Boys are said to be more casual in their approach towards life. They forget the little things that happen in day-to-day life and are more focused on the main picture or the bigger issues of life. Whereas, girls stick to every incident and overthink about it. It's their characteristic that cannot be changed. So for a woman, her girlfriends are the most important ones who play the part of keeping them sane. They help her understand and reason out what may have been the motive behind it. It's something that makes her relate to and suddenly it all makes sense and thus relaxes her brain.

> *"Friendship is born at that moment when one person says to another, 'What! You too? I thought I was the only one."*
>
> C.S. Lewis

Many of us are in the mind-set that the longer we are friends with someone, the better friends we are. I don't believe this to be true. We can say when two people stay connected for longer, the bond become stronger, but this doesn't mean that the person we have just met cannot be the real friend we were in search of. It just simply clicks. The bond feels strong from the very beginning and our thinking will match.

Two people may be completely different from each other, in many aspects of life. What truly connects friends is the comfort level each one feels in the presence of the other, respect and love. The importance we hold in the other person's life is what makes the bond stronger. We may not realise immediately who are our friends, but time will make it clear.

> *"A single rose can be my garden… a single friend, my world."*
>
> Leo Buscaglia

Once you find such a friend, hold on to the soul for life and see how beautiful life is.

Was It Love???

Photo by Aziz Acharki on Unsplash

One fine morning, in early June, I landed at a new city, where I would be pursuing my college. My mother had come along with me to get me settled, since, it was the first time I was about to live away from home, and the thought itself had been freaking them for months.

We had arrived a few days before the college was due to start, and she took this opportunity to make me meet the few people she knew there. One of her friend's sons was also starting his college here, so she took me to introduce me to them. *'Just in case of emergencies'* – she said, trying to convince me, as I rolled my eyes. I had not even known about her this friend's existence and so I wasn't comfortable with this introduction thing.

Finally, we arrived at their hotel. The boy's mother opened the door and the introductions started. The boy was busy unpacking his luggage when his mother called him to introduce us. My first look on seeing him was that he was cute. The elders asked us to exchange our mobile numbers so that we may be in touch, but since we were yet to purchase a local SIM, we came to the conclusion that we would take it from our respective mothers, if the need be. Then we left, as even I had a lot of stuff to do before college would start.

My mother went back home after two days and I moved to the hostel, ready to attend college the next day.

College was good. Soon I made friends in college as well as in hostel. It was a different experience altogether, living with girls of your age. It was fun. Each of us had so much to share and days passed swiftly.

On one such day, we were playing truth and dare at our hostel late at night, when my phone beeped. There was a message from an unknown number saying- *"Hey this is*

John. You had come to my hotel with your mother. If you don't remember, kindly ignore this message".

It took me a second to realise it was my mother's friend's son. I had actually not bothered to ask his name that day as I was too embarrassed. I was pleasantly surprised and to an extent, flattered. I had found him cute and had wanted to stay in touch, but was too shy to admit. Now that he had messaged me from his new number, somehow it made me feel good that he remembered me. I quickly replied that of-course I do remember him. I saved his number and from that day we started to chat via messages.

In those days we didn't have WhatsApp and SMS were the only messaging option. Being a student then, we got a good deal of 100 free SMS per day. This was to our advantage, as, during college life, we had to limit our expenses.

At first, our chats were restricted to 'Hello, how was your day?' and those formal stuffs. Slowly, as we got more open to each other, the number of messages we exchanged, increased, and it slowly reached the point where we would exhaust our daily limit of 100 SMS and would have to wait for it to be past 12 a.m. so that our message pack would be re-activated.

My friends would complain that I was always on phone, but I wouldn't bother. He had become a good friend of mine, though I didn't understand if my feelings for him meant more than that. I wasn't ready to accept. I had a soft corner for him, but I didn't know how he felt about me. Our chats were always casual.

We used to be the first ones to wish each other on birthdays and our friends would tease us mercilessly. We met rarely and when we did, it was just a friendly meet. I knew my feelings for him were getting stronger by the day, but I was scared to voice it out. What if he only thought me to be a good friend? He was cute and handsome, of-course he would want to have hotter girls as his girlfriends. I didn't want to face rejection and lose him even as a friend.

Days passed into months and finally it was our vacation time. I was heading home after 6 whole months and was damn excited. His college didn't have vacation that time and I knew it won't be possible to message him, till the duration I was at home.

On my way back from home, I was travelling on a train with one of my hostel friend. In the train we meet a guy who was very helpful and sweet. That night as soon as I reached back to my hostel, the first thing I did was message John.

His response was prompt, as if he had been waiting for my message. It was flattering as I had missed messaging and chatting with him. After we updated each other about the last few days, he suddenly asked me if I had a crush on someone. I was confused as to why was he asking me this now. Still, I thought to play it a little and said about the guy I met on the train. His response was an abrupt 'Ok', for which I didn't know what to reply. Within seconds I got another message from him asking me to sleep as I must be tired from all the travelling. It was then I realised how tired I was, and so took his advice and slept off.

Next day I didn't hear from him till noon. On asking, he just said that he was busy with a project which he had to submit in a few days. Though I did feel there was something wrong, I didn't push him further and decided I would only message him next when he did. For the next few days I didn't hear from him. When it was no longer possible for me to control myself, I finally gave up and messaged him if there was something bothering him. He replied after an hour saying that he had already told me that he was busy with the project.

I was hurt and confused. Why was he behaving like this? Was he jealous of the train guy? If he did have feeling for me, why didn't he ever say me in all these months? And was this reason enough to break all that we had?

Slowly our communication became almost negligible till it reached a point where we only wished each other on birthdays.

As the years passed, my marriage got fixed and my ring ceremony was decided to be held at my home town. After the engagement, as we were having dinner with all our guests, someone patted me on my back. When I turned, I saw John standing there. Seeing my perplexed expression, he explained that since I hadn't bothered calling him on my great day, he decided he would still come and convey his regards in person.

I was happy to see him, but also sad and nervous as if someone had caught me committing some crime. It still wasn't clear what made him so detached from me. Was it really my fault? What would my life had been if that one incident hadn't taken place?

It's been 5 years now since I got married. He is also married now to his love, whom he met when he started working after college. We still wish each other on birthdays and other special occasions, just like friends do.

But were we ever anything more than friends? Did he ever share the same feelings that I had for him? Had there ever been love between us? Don't lovers always meet in the end and live happily ever after? I still don't know.

But as they say, *life goes on and life isn't a fairy-tale.*

Photo by Matteo Vistocco on Unsplash

Self-Importance Is Important

Nobody will care for you enough

Finally weekend is here. It's Saturday morning and I am already tensed about what I should wear tonight at the party. All my husband's friends are going to be there with all the ladies decked up as if they have just been out of some fashion show. I need to look my best. I finally finalised on a short off-shoulder black dress with red pumps.

Soon it was night and before I know, we are at the party. As always, the party starts with drinks. I order my usual cocktail because I still haven't gotten used to the taste of any beer or wine. I never used to drink before marriage, but here, as everyone talks and sways their glasses, I force myself to drink it. But, even after these 5 years I hate it. I hate its taste, I hate how it makes me feel, but to be socially accepted, I have to. I don't want to be looked down upon.

We all have, at some point in time, forced our self to do something just because everyone else does, and we feel if we don't follow, we won't be socially accepted or will be tagged as a boring person. We give more importance to other people's thoughts over ourselves. What we don't understand, in the words of Mark Twain, is -

"A man cannot be comfortable without his own approval."

We forget that what other people think of us should not be our concern. If we start thinking what others will think about us, what will the 'others' think about? Don't we have more important things to do and think of? We can't change what others think about us, so why bother? Everyone has their own opinions. We can't make others to think our way. And frankly, nobody has time to waste, thinking about a third person. In today's fast paced world, we don't even have a minute to wander.

So, it's time to stop worrying about others and start thinking about our own self. We need to make our self the first priority because nobody is going to stay forever with us. When we fall ill, our close ones may provide us with the best medication and comfort, but we have to bear the pain and suffering. Nobody can help us with that or even help reduce it a tiny bit.

Our life is our own and we need to walk through this path of life alone. The good deeds done by others won't help us. We need to create our own mark. For that we need to spend more time understanding our self, finding out what we are good at and working on developing that skill.

Our life is what we make of it. The more importance we give to our health, loving our self and perfecting our talent, the easier life will be on us.

> *"You yourself, as much as anybody in the entire universe, deserve your love and affection"*
>
> Buddha

Having lots of friends is not an achievement; instead, we should focus of having few real ones. Even if we have a single real friend, believe me that will be the greatest achievement of our life.

By saying we should give most importance to our own self, I don't mean we shouldn't treat others well. What I mean is that, we need to do what is good for others and ourselves. We shouldn't harm our self in order to please others. Real friend help us achieve this. They are the ones who will bring out the best in us.

On the other hand, too much self-importance will destroy us. It's like termites, eating us away from the inside without us even knowing. Nobody likes to be in the company of someone who always boasts about themselves. If we give too much self-importance to ourselves, slowly people will start drifting away from us and we will be left all alone. This loneliness slowly leads to depression, and depression may also lead to a person's death.

Self-importance should be a quality that others admire in us, not something that drives people away.

This is correctly described in the words of Lucille Ball -

> *"Love yourself first and everything else falls into line. You really have to love yourself to get anything done in this world."*

Every morning, stand in front of the mirror and say these three magical words to yourself - "I Love You", and see how life changes for the best.

Photo by Tim Mossholder on Unsplash

Men vs. Women

Are they treated equally?

When you travel with a guy, who is expected to carry the heavier luggage? If only a single seat is available in a bus/metro, between a man and a woman, who is expected to give the seat to the other? When you go to a restaurant with your man, who is expected to pay the bills? Isn't it men most of the times?

In today's world, where women are supposed to be given equal status as men, we should also note that this equality should work both ways. By saying this I mean, women should be thought to be no less than men in emotional, mental or physical aspect.

Women should be given equal opportunity to grow professionally, but on the other hand, women should not be given more priority when it comes to day to day life, as in, for example, reserved seats for ladies in buses and metros. Women should not be considered weaker than men physically.

The main responsibility of providing for all the needs of a family is always on the man of the house. Why can't a woman be equally responsible for providing for the family? Won't two earning hands be better than one?

The advantages this will have are:

- It will lessen his burden
- He will be able to spend more time with family.

It's a win-win situation. When he has more time to spend with family, he can help his wife with household chores as well, thus reducing the stress of the woman and make it more enjoyable.

Why does any work need to be termed to be for either for a man or a woman? There shouldn't be any pre-defined tasks for men and women. It should be based on an individual's strengths and capabilities, rather than gender. Gender of a person should be inconsequential.

Men also need to change the way they think. They should not think themselves to be the superior being and let go of 'Men's Ego'. It's fine if a woman pays at a restaurant, it doesn't really matter. If a woman is as strong as the man, what's the harm in lifting the luggage? Why should household chores be a women's job and providing for the family, a men's? It should be based on who is better at what.

Parents should start teaching their children this important concept of equality. Involve them in indoor and outdoor activities irrespective of their gender. Focus on their interest and help them perfect it as that will take them places.

Why should a girl always leave her home and move-in with the boy and his family after marriage? Aren't the girl's parents equally important for her? For it to be equal for both, parents should let their children move out and live on their own. Even the boy should understand what a girl goes through when she leaves her near and dear ones after she gets married. This way both will be able to understand each other better as both are in the same phase of life. Moreover it will help them face the difficulties of life together making them emotionally strong.

Based on study, since 2012, more and more women are taking part in Olympics and currently the number is almost 50 percentages as compared to men. This proves that women are no lesser than men.

As an individual, we should try and get this change in our day-to-day life as well. It's our fault of we expect others to be considerate towards us only because we are women. If we want equality of men and women, we need to first believe ourselves to be equal to men. We should start breaking the false stereotypes of the world and contribute in implementing this change.

Don't look for others to bring the change. Be the change and the world will follow.

Photo by Unknown

Are You A Good Listener?

The key to great communication

One day I was attending a seminar. The topic for the day was "How to lead a quality life?" The speaker had the attention of all the guests and he was doing a very good job of explaining each tip with an example of how we could implement it in our lives.

The seminar was to last for 6 long hours, but the speaker had us so engrossed that we didn't realise the hours pass by. Soon the seminar came to an end and the speaker announced that he was open for questions.

The first person stood and started his question saying "You are a liar...", but before he could complete his sentence, the speaker became furious, and started insulting the person. The organizers had to intrude. The person was then asked why he said that and that he should apologise. The person then clarified that all he wanted to ask was "You are a liar. If someone accuses you of this, how do you stay calm?"

Here we see, though the speaker was a good communicator, but he lacked listening skills. He jumped to conclusion before the person could finish his question. This way he affected his own reputation.

What is communication?

Communication is a two-way process which consists of two main components:

- Speak
- Listen

For it to be a fruitful communication, all the parties involved must have both of these skills. Communication cannot happen with only one speaking and the other just listening.

There are many books and articles on how we can improve our speaking skills; however, the importance of listening skills is mostly ignored. It requires a good amount of patience and concentration. Just like we need a great amount of practice to be a great speaker, listening requires the same (even more in some cases) effort.

At any point in time, we have a number of thoughts running in our minds. This is the main cause which prevents a person to be a good listener. We need to train our mind to focus on what is being said and put the other thoughts in the back stack.

Importance of Listening

Listening skills are required on our day to day life. Let's take a very simple example.

We all have given some sort of interviews in our lives. Be it a job interview or even when we meet the parents' of the person we want to marry. In such cases we are nervous and we have a single chance to create an impression on the interviewer, so we want to make the most of it.

Doesn't it happen many a times that we start answering even before listening to the entire question? This is like digging our own graves. So, the first impression that we have unintentionally created is, that we lack listening skills. This may result in rejection, because this is a very important virtue a person is expected to have.

This is not the only scenario. Simple instances of our life, like going to a restaurant with our partner or a friend. Our mind maybe pre-occupied with various thoughts while the other person might be sharing some important instance of its life. This result in the other person feeling ignored, unimportant or even insulted. Next time you will be deprived of this person's company, no matter how much they truly meant to you.

So, cultivate your listening skills, as this is one of the main skills of a successful person.

> *"Of all the skills of leadership, listening is the most valuable – and one of the least understood. Most captains of industry listen only sometimes, and they remain ordinary leaders. But a few, the great ones, never stop listening. That's how they get word before anyone else of unseen problems and opportunities."*

Peter Nulty, Fortune Magazine

Photo by Tom Pumford on Unsplash

Boys Don't Cry

If only they knew, boys have emotions too!!!

When we watch some emotional cinema, and at the end, if any of the boys are found crying, the first thing we hear people laugh about is 'He is crying like a girl'. This is because we are not used to seeing a boy cry.

Based on research, boys are said to be emotionally weaker. A girl of the same age is more matured as compared to a boy. Then why do we have this stereotype? Does it even sound logical?

Being a girl, I get attracted to boys who cry, as it displays his emotional side. After all, will we want our partner to be emotionless?

Since the time a boy is a born, he is always made to believe that he is not supposed to cry. What I don't understand is what the harm in crying is? Why can't a boy express that he is hurt? It will only lighten his heart. We can only help a person we know is suffering. If we hide our emotions, the other person may not know, and it will instead harm our own self. These feelings pile up and our behaviour may change. This will drive people further away.

Someone has rightly said – Boys don't cry but real men do...

Crying should not be seen as a sign of weakness, instead it's a sign of strength. It is the body's mechanism to cope with pain.

Based on research, in addition to being self-soothing, shedding emotional tears releases certain hormones in the human body which makes people feel good and may also ease both physical and emotional pain. In this way, crying can help reduce pain and promote a sense of well-being.

So, be a Man and don't be ashamed to display your emotions. Laugh when you are happy, cry when you are sad. Isn't this what babies do? And babies are believed to be a version of God. So never kill the baby within you.

Be like a child, but not childish.

Do You Know How Talented You Are?

Photo by Joel Valve on Unsplash

Remember when we were in school, many a times our teachers used to make us write good and bad point about ourselves, in a sheet of paper? Based on my experience, I observed, most of us always had more bad points as compared to the good ones.

Why do we underestimate ourselves? We admire others for various things, but when it comes to ourselves, we feel we are not as talented as compared to the other. This is so not true.

God has given each one of us some or the other unique quality or talent, which we may not even be aware of (believe me as this is by personal experience). And you know what? We will come to know about this talent at some point in time when we most need it, that's the mystery of life.

> *In the words of George Lucas – "Everybody has talent, it's just a matter of moving around until you've discovered what it is."*

So, we just need to keep doing our best and, most importantly, know who we are. We need to love ourselves before we can truly love others. This also reciprocates. Only when we love ourselves, will others love us. Others see the good what we see in ourselves.

Think about this: if there is a person who always speaks low of itself, would you love spending time with the person?? After a certain point of time, you wouldn't right? This is because when we are negative about ourselves, we create a negative aura around us which drives people away.

What we can do is, instead of hating ourselves for anything, we should try and work on it and improve it.

And the good we see in ourselves, we need to cultivate it as that's our strength.

God has chosen you and sent you to this world, isn't this special in itself? God loves you, and so should you.

Photo by Sydney Sims on Unsplash

How To Deal With A Person

Suffering From Depression

In today's world, we see that the number of people suffering from depression has increased significantly. People are getting aware of what is depression, but do we know how to deal with a person who is suffering from depression?

The main key is to understand its cause. We may list a number of reasons that may lead to depression, but the main cause is 'Insecurity'.

The world is getting more competitive by the day, and everyone needs to battle beyond their capabilities to survive. From a child to an adult, we all are competing to be better than the other. A child securing 90% in its boards is also insecure, as there are several others who will score higher and get first preference at the best schools and colleges.

Everyone wants to be on top. What we forget is that only a single person may be at the top, but what we must also remember is that those who are below, are equally competent and it is a mere chance that the other person is at the top. We all are unique and are good at something or the other. Our aim must be to compete with ourselves, to be better than what we were yesterday. We need to discover what we are good at. 'Do your best' should be the mantra. If a fish is asked to climb a tree and is judged on its capability to climb a tree, it will always believe itself to be dumb.

The best medicine for depression is - to make the person feel secure, make them believe that they are doing their best and we are proud of them. Help the person see what all they have achieved is worthwhile.

People lose confidence in themselves when they are depressed. This is why we should always compliment people for anything good they have done. It's not hard, is it?

They may behave in a particular manner, don't judge by what they are doing, instead, go deep, and try to reason why they are doing this. We need to have patience, as the person is already going through a number of conflicting emotions. We need to make them feel we are there for them, no matter what. Although, it is extremely difficult not to get perturbed, but that is what makes us a better person. Perseverance is the key.

So, don't keep anything in your heart. Speak out if you are hurt, compliment others and accept when others compliment you, love yourself and accept what you have achieved is best for you. If one door closes, God will always open the next one for you and life goes on, no matter what.

Is Money Everything??

Photo by Alexander Grey on Unsplash

We must have come across this question at least once in our lifetime. What do you think? If we have money, do we have everything? In other words, can money buy everything we desire or dream of?

To an extent we may say 'Yes'; we may buy the best house at the best location, eat the best food or get the best medical treatment available. What more can we ask for? We may argue that money can't buy love, but in most of the cases today, we do see that if a person loves someone dearly, but doesn't have enough money to live a comfortable life, it is not always true that the other person will be ready to sacrifice everything for love. But is money seriously everything is a debatable question.

We ruin our health at the prime stage of our life by running after money, and the rest of our life, we lose the hard earned money on trying to rectify our health. Why can't we see this simple truth and lead a more meaningful life?

We just have one life; shouldn't we be living it to the fullest? We should work hard, no doubt, but why not even spend some of the money we earn in enjoying life while we have the time. We should try and balance our work and personal life as both are equally important. Be considerable towards our health as, in the end, that's what stays with us. Old and sick is a dreadful combination.

In today's world everyone is competing with the other, everyone wants to earn more and more money. What we forget is, even if we have all the wealth of the world, we cannot use all of it. We cannot take the money with us to our graves. This money is valid only till we are in this world, and this time is restricted. We don't know what will happen tomorrow. Saving for the future, isn't it a little too much to think about now, when we don't even know if we will be able to see tomorrow's Sun?

So, we should start living for today. Saying this, I don't mean we shouldn't save at all, but just have enough that will help us to continue living our life with ease. Why do we have to save for our kids? Don't we have the confidence in them that they can earn for their own? A parent's job is to provide good education to their kids and make them capable enough to care for themselves. Their job ends there. Then they should let their kids discover themselves on their own. Face the hurdles the path of life throws on them. It will only make them stronger.

Spend time with your loved ones. If you are busy earning money throughout your life, maybe to keep your loved ones with great comfort, but what if they are not there tomorrow to even experience it? You may not even get time to show how much they mattered to you, because you were so busy with your work. Maybe it's your company that they actually yearn for, and not all the comforts of the world? So express them your feelings when you have the time. Let them feel they are loved by spending time with them, and not by just providing for all their needs.

The richest person of the world may not be the happiest, or the poorest person of the world may not be the most depressed. Money is addictive. The more you have it, the more you want. Our body is such that it may even survive in the harshest of conditions, but the more comfort we provide it, the more used to it becomes. It's like dough; we may mould it the way we want.

On the other side, we may also say that money can buy life. If a person is ill and doesn't receive proper treatment due to the lack of money, it may lose its life, whereas, a person with money may get the right treatment and survive.

So, money is not everything, but it is surely an integral part of our life. Still, why should we not live life like there is no tomorrow.

Photo by Daniel Lincoln on Unsplash

Sometimes a push is all you need

It was Diwali time in India - The festival of lights as they call it. This is the time when the whole country is lit up and everyone is celebrating it with their near and dear ones. It is said these lights drive away the evil so all the houses are beautifully lit.

The office was already getting empty with all employees going on vacation. I too wanted to take a vacation and go home to spend some time with my family, but something was stopping me. I was scared my manager would not approve my leaves. I was scared of rejection.

Just then, as one of my colleagues was getting ready to leave for the day, he asked me what my Diwali plans were. I simply shrugged and said, "Come to office and work". He seemed shocked at my response. He asked why I was not going home. I hesitantly said that the manager won't approve with so many already on leave.

It was then he told me those golden words, "How do you know when you have not even asked him yet. At least give it a try before you come to any conclusion". These words just stuck me at the right place and it made so much sense. I did give it a try, and the next thing I know was I was on a flight to my native to spend the festival with my family. It was just the "little push" I needed.

Doesn't this happen with most of us? We come to conclusion before even giving it a try, just because we are scared of rejection. What we don't understand is how we will even be able to taste success if we are not ready to face failure. If we only do a thing we are 100% confident of succeeding, will this success taste as sweet as when we succeed in something we have really tired hard for.

In the words of C. S. Lewis –

> *Failures, repeated failures, are finger posts on the road to achievement. One fails forward toward success*

So don't wait for that little push from any external source. That push should be from within you, as unlike that one instance, we may not always receive the "push" at the right time and we may miss an opportunity that was laid for us.

Don't be scared of rejection, be scared of not trying.

YOU!!!

Photo by Etty Fidele on Unsplash

You are just amazing!! How many times have people told you this? Maybe when you help them with something or accomplished something the other person didn't. It sounds great right? But how many times have you said this to yourself?

Most of the times, we are so busy appreciating others, that we forget our own achievements. We never compliment ourselves. We don't acknowledge the hurdles that we have crossed in life.

Everyone has their own life with their own set of hurdles which they need to overcome. Don't ever compare yourself with others. You may think how well established your school mate or college mate is, but what you forget is their path of life is different as compared to yours. Be confident that whatever you have done so far is what is best for you.

I don't say we shouldn't aspire to become like someone, but we should just try and do our best. In the end, what we achieve is what we deserved and we should learn to be satisfied with it. We should be sure that we have put in our 100% and this is what is best for us as our path of life may not always lead us to that of our role model.

Each one of us are unique in the best possible way, so start loving yourself and the problems of life will seem to vanish.

Be who YOU are. YOU are the best version of yourself and YOU are amazing.